The Motivating Leader

Lewis Losoncy is the director of the Institute for Personal and Organizational Development in Reading, Pennsylvania. He has lectured on motivation and encouragement management to small businesses, schools, universities, and large corporations in more than forty states and most of Canada. He is the author of *You Can Do It!: How to Encourage Yourself* and *Turning People On: How to Be an Encouraging Person* and the co-author of *The Encouragement Book: Becoming a Positive Person.*

The *Motivating Leader*

Lewis Losoncy

PRENTICE HALL PRESS • NEW YORK

Published in 1986 by Prentice Hall Press
A Division of Simon & Schuster, Inc.
Gulf + Western Building
One Gulf + Western Plaza
New York, NY 10023

Originally published by Prentice-Hall, Inc.

PRENTICE HALL PRESS is a trademark of Simon & Schuster, Inc.

Library of Congress Cataloging-in-Publication Data

Losoncy, Lewis E.
    The motivating leader.

    Bibliography: p.
    Includes index.
    1. Leadership.   2. Achievement motivation.
3. Performance.   I. Title.
BF637.L4L59   1985   658.3'14   84-17766
ISBN 0-13-603846-8
ISBN 0-13-603838-7 (pbk.)

Manufactured in the United States of America

10 9 8 7 6 5 4 3

First Prentice Hall Press Edition

Contents

Introduction, 1

1
The Encouraging Leader, ~~23~~ 6

2
Insights to Make You
a Motivating Leader, ~~6~~ 23

3
Positive Leadership Approaches
to Resolve Differences, 41

4
The Motivating Leader
Is a People Builder, 60

5

Plant Positive Purpose in People, 82

6

Create a Winning Feeling, 97

7

Confront with Class, 112

8

Put Your People in Second Gear, 139

9

Erase Apathy and Uncooperativeness, 162

10

Turn Individuals
into Team Players, 176

Practical Applications, 190

Glossary, 195

Bibliography, 202

Index, 207

Acknowledgments

To my mother and father, who believed that you "raised" children by picking them up, not putting them down.

To my friend Dick Cahn, who believed that more than anything else the leader must be able to inspire and trust the people in the organization. No wonder he has earned the reputation of being one of the most knowledgeable educational leaders on the topic of improving school morale in the United States.

To Lynne Lumsden, editor-in-chief of the General Publishing Division of Prentice-Hall, who believed in the importance of encouragement even when it was unfashionable and went on to publish a half dozen books on the topic.

To Dean Karrel, the best marketing person I ever met, who convinced me of the need for *The Motivating Leader.* I thank him for his enthusiastic style coupled with his facts that "almost every single leader or manager in small businesses, schools, government, or even in the family or classroom has never had any practical training in how to motivate others and just plows through the day on hope." This book is designed to be an alternative to what Dean called "The Leadership School of Hard Knocks."

To all of the members of the North American Society of Adlerian Psychology, a spirited group of optimists, who believe that if there are two ways of getting a job done, why not choose the most positive way?

And to *you*, with this simple insight: Isn't it interesting that you never see a pessimistic, nitpicking, cynical, or negative influence in the acknowledgments of any book? Why do you think that might be?

With love to Pam and Shauna—the ones who motivate the motivator.

The Motivating Leader

Introduction

It was said that Walt Disney could wring out the creativity from his artists' minds long after they themselves thought that their ideas had dried up. One could say that he helped people go a step beyond to make Fantasyland a real place on a map. John Kennedy had the ability to motivate a nation of people to ask what they could do for their land. Mother Theresa inspired the world by giving nourishment to the hearts of its people. Martin Luther King, Jr., added some new dimensions to the way a society looks at itself.

These leaders and many others had something in common. They had the ability to move people to greater achievements, to appeal to the highest motives in people, and to help everyone feel like an involved, contributing team member. And their leadership techniques are relevant to all who are in roles where their own success depends on their ability to influence others to action.

Whether you call yourself a leader, a manager, a coach, a parent, an administrator, or a president, or even if you feel like a shepherd with a flock, your most important resource is your people. And the most crucial determinant of success—reaching your goal—is your ability to influence, inspire, motivate, and encourage your human resources.

Those who have the talent to call others to committed action are often referred to as "born leaders." But they weren't born leaders the day they entered the world. No, as leaders they were born the day they developed the skills to get in tune with their people, the techniques to turn on the unmotivated, the knowledge to inspire the irresponsible, and the art of lifting up the down and bringing in the out. The Disneys, the Kennedys, and the others did not have a monopoly on how to motivate others. Everyone who learns and uses these techniques of motivating through encouragement can begin a whole new refreshing life as a leader. You can become a motivating leader. Happy Birthday!

Why Do Leaders Fail?
And How Can They Succeed?

A skilled haircutter was promoted to the position of managing a twelve-person beauty salon. With an excellent formal background in styling hair and some on-the-job training in specific areas such as budgeting, retailing, and appointment scheduling, she eagerly faced her new challenge. It wasn't long after she received her manager nametag that the people part of her job started to whittle away her will. She lacked skills in leadership and assertiveness with people, and the salon personnel started to tread all over her like an un—welcome mat. The stress that her lack of people skills caused was transformed into psychological symptoms. Insomnia, anxiety attacks, and frequent headaches were as much a part of her life as her job. After a period of only four months, the formerly successful cosmetologist left not only her management position but her profession.

This sad story could have been rewritten if this manager had developed:

1. a take-charge attitude toward her people to gain their cooperation and respect

2. a strategy to minimize employee problems through setting up policies and procedures

3. a systematic approach to constructively steer problem employees onto the constructive path

4. encouragement to keep her head up and even enjoy the challenge of managing people.

The ambitious middle-aged manager of a fast-food restaurant supervises mostly young adults in her seven-day-a-week operation. She can't believe the irresponsibility she sees in her minimum-wage employees. Latenesses or absences are almost daily occurrences, and she is at her wit's end in trying to find a way to motivate these kids to take on more responsibility. The well-intentioned leader argues that "kids nowadays don't want to work like we did back when."

So the fast-food manager needs to develop her new skills in motivating the youngsters of today. The fast-food restaurant manager needs to develop:

1. approaches to encourage her young workers to be responsible, motivated, and productive employees

2. a plan to help her people not only deal with everyday problems but to learn to anticipate other possible problems

3. skills in hiring new employees and skills to tackle the task of firing if the time comes.

A husband and wife recently signed up to start their own family business on a part-time (and, they hoped, someday full-time) basis. They believe firmly in the product, they know it's the best, and they want to spread their fervor to everyone. They get some people enthused to become involved, but they find that people soon burn out and get turned off. They begin to realize that their success in the business is related to not just a knowledge of that product but also skills in understanding and motivating people. This couple's business *could* have achieved booming success had they developed:

1. an approach to win people over

2. skills in building responsible self-starters who can function without constantly being prodded

3. a system to build pride in their people to increase productivity.

The spirited salesperson moves up the ranks like a helium balloon under water to the position of sales manager. This highly competitive manager argues that the way to motivate people is to play one person against another. Constantly highlighting the top person's sales performance with charts, public recognition, and free vacations, the manager believes that this is the way to get all the people "moving." After all, the competitive strategy worked with her. And it does work with about 15 percent of the people. On what appears to be a side note, the sales manager notices backbiting, sabotaging, jealousy, excessive excuse making, and poor morale in most of the salespeople. She wonders why the people won't work together, cooperate, and teach one another their sales techniques that work.

With some practical help, the sales manager could have developed:

1. a plan to build team power whereby everyone works together as a cooperative helpful unit
2. a strategy to increase the sales productivity of all people, not just a few
3. approaches to encourage a desire on everyone's part to channel competitive energies where they belong—against the competitive companies—not against one another.

The high school coach, a talented strategist and himself an excellent athlete in his early years, doesn't understand why his players are so apathetic. He has used the Lombardi hard-nosed approach with them and lost two of his top players who said, "We don't need this grief." He switched to the soft approach and is convinced that he lost the team's respect. The coach doesn't know where to turn, but he knows that unless he improves morale and his win–loss record, he won't be asked back the following year. The coach can improve his skills in leading his people if he develops:

1. an understanding of how to get people motivated to give their best

2. self-confidence to be a goal-centered, not an ego-centered ("I must be boss") coach

3. skills in building a team spirit with high morale.

Yes, the manager of the salon, the manager of the fast-food restaurant, the husband and wife who had the family business, the sales manager, and the coach all had many assets that elevated them to their positions. But they soon found themselves in positions in which their success depended on the performance of others. New skills—skills in understanding and motivating other people—were demanded. And, unfortunately, most leaders have never received this training.

That training is the mission of The Motivating Leader.

The Encouraging Leader

Have you ever noticed how you can sense the style of a leader just by observing the attitudes of a few of the employees?

It's true! Just as the floating leaves of fall hint of the presence of nearby trees, the attitudes of the people in an organization (whether it be a business, a team, or a family) whisper about the leader's style. Each day provides tons of opportunities for you to subtly observe the results of a leader's "way of being."

Imagine that you have just quivered through a stormy five-hour coast-to-coast flight. Your body is still shaking like a tuning fork as you await the faceless limo driver from Hotel Unknown located in a city that has never lived in the cozy areas of your mind. Your comfortable feelings are as lost as your baggage. The driver from the hotel finally arrives, steps out of the van, and greets you with a big ear-to-ear smile. His warm, helpful actions overpower some of the chill of the evening. The enthusiastic youth is telling you by his very "way of being" the theme that the hotel manager has instilled within him

Next, you experience the help of the cheerful, courteous woman at the hotel registration desk. By her positive attitude, she is prophesying a pleasant visit for you while nesting in her employer's spaces.

This team of the limo driver and the clerk are your first samples, your leading clues that the hotel is customer-oriented. Your senses, explosive from the hectic pace, are delicately detonated by employee empathy. Your out-of-town anxieties lose their argument. The crystal ball in your mind tells you that you can kick off your shoes and relax. You get that "new bed sheet feeling" in your home away from home.

The hotel is no longer a stranger to you because of its motivated people. And you can be certain of one fact: these winning employee attitudes did not happen haphazardly. The positive people atmosphere is the result of a hotel manager, "the hero behind the scenes," who knows how to motivate people to become productive employees. The leader's style makes the difference!

The manager's style is the unparalleled reason why employees are involved in developing and sharing better, more efficient, or more creative ideas. Most organizations, clubs, businesses, teams, and families have so many human resources in their ranks to find new ways of solving problems, to envision the creation of fresh ideas, or to conceive of more effective ways of achieving goals than is realized. Whether these human resources are tapped, and whether the members feel involved or courageous enough to share their ideas are directly related to the leader's style.

In a discouraging atmosphere employees hold their ideas—as children do when they fear raising their hands at school in the presence of a discouraging teacher. On the contrary, in an encouraging atmosphere creative ideas and suggestions for improvement flow like the high tide.

The employees of a novelty manufacturing company meet with the manager with the goal of generating ideas for future products. There certainly isn't a lack of ideas present in the employees' minds but they may very well lack the courage to express those ideas.

"Should I share my new thought today, or would the manager make a sarcastic, discouraging comment about its merits?" Many employees wonder. Red and green lights flash on intermittently in the creative employee's mind and heart based on more than anything else, the person's perceptions of the manager's "way of being."

The smiling manager asserts, "Remember, the only bad idea today is the one that isn't shared. The idea sitting in your mind right now could be the big one, the cornerstone for our company's future. At worst, the idea won't be able to be used at this time. There is no downside risk to expressing your creative thoughts."

An anxious employee, now encouraged by the manager's style raises his hand and says, "Well, I have this idea about creating a toy that would be cheap to manufacture, easy to package, and is novel. You see, I call this new toy a 'pet rock.' It could ..."

The manager's style makes the difference!!

What Can the Encouraging Leader Accomplish?

Why be an encouraging, motivating leader? There are eight primary goals that encouraging leaders can more effectively achieve through his or her people that discouraging leadership doesn't—or does only on the short term.

Goal 1: The encouraging leader creates an atmosphere of mutual understanding and respect for each member's responsibilities and roles (Aren't misunderstandings and disrespect the primary reasons for disharmony)? or (Why doesn't the chef appreciate the waitress)?

Goal 2: The encouraging leader builds team members by being a positive influence who recognizes their potential (Discouraging leaders actually believe you build people up by tearing them down.)

Goal 3: The encouraging leader combats burn-out and lifts people out of the rut by giving meaning to what they do. (Discouraging leaders assume that a paycheck is the only reason people work and miss out on so much people potential.)

Goal 4: The encouraging leader increases productivity by conveying positive expectations or a "we can do

8

it" feeling. (Did you ever have a leader who had no confidence in you and your abilities? How did you perform?)

Goal 5: The encouraging leader has the skills to constructively steer the problem person back on the productive path. (Discouraging leaders use the name-calling, shouting path because it works sometimes . . . temporarily.)

Goal 6: The encouraging leader is a realist . . . and an optimist who faces the realistic challenges head-on and mobilizes the human resources to find the solutions. (Discouraging leaders make the mistake of either "wishing things be different" or "believing that the problems have no answers.")

Goal 7: The encouraging leader skillfully knows how to tap the creative minds of the team members. (Discouraging leaders squash ideas with "that'll never work here" or "you must be *kidding!*")

Goal 8: The encouraging leader has the talent to turn self-centered individuals into team players. (Discouraging leaders highlight individuals and emphasize competition over cooperation and sacrifice team spirit.)

You can be the Motivating Leader who draws the ideas from many sources. The primary influence is Alfred Adler, the psychiatrist of optimism who believed that human behavior can best be understood in its "social context." Have you ever performed at two different levels of productivity with two different leaders? If so, it was probably because of the way you were led by this other person in your "social setting."

Adler believed that people's primary needs were to be "noticed," to be "significant," to be "contributors," and "to belong." The encouraging leader can help people meet those social needs and thus they can be fulfilled on the team, family or in the workplace. (Indeed, our research at People Media, Inc., a Reading, Pennsylvania based educational research firm, validates the social needs of people. One questionnaire resulted in almost 80 percent of the respondents saying, "I work for more than the money—I work for my manager's recognition.")

Another influence on encouragement leadership was

9

psychologist Abraham Maslow, who studied the healthiest people whom he called self-actualizers. He questioned the old way of studying people with the emphasis on disease and asked instead, "How high can people reach—what are their ceilings?" The encouraging leader tries to create those conditions in the organization, team, or family to bring out the best in the human resources. As inventor Henry Kirn says, "There are two types of leaders—the gardener and the horticulturist. The gardener thinks small, the horticulturist thinks big." The encouraging leader is a horticulturist who grows people to reach for their ceilings.

Along with Adler and Maslow some influences on encouraging leadership have been Dale Carnegie, Carl Rogers, William Glasser, Albert Ellis, Douglas McGregor and William Ouchi. But the key influences were the every-day leaders I consulted with who already knew in their very viscera about encouragement and discouragement. And you the reader already know much about what encourages and discourages people from your own experiences.

To prove that you know about discouragement, take just two minutes and experience a simple exercise on what behaviors discourage people.

Your Exercise to Identify the Characteristics
of Discouraging Leaders

Think of the most discouraging leader, manager, boss, supervisor, teacher, or foreman you ever experienced. When you have identified the person, list at least five characteristics, traits or 'ways of being' that this person exhibited that discouraged you. Make your responses either global, for example, this person never listened to me, or specific, for example, when I started on the job he or she didn't even introduce me to anyone. List your answers below. If you find more than five, feel free to add.

1. _____

2. _____

3. _____

4. _____

5. _____

_____

Below I have listed some responses I received from leaders to this same question you just answered. Do your responses match any of theirs?

These are Responses from people to the question: "What were some of the characteristics of the most *discouraging* leader you experienced?" (Responses are recorded *exactly* as they were given.)

1. Always pointed out what I was doing wrong, never what I did right.

2. Never listened.

3. Had double standards, one for his favorites—another for other people.

4. Know it all.

5. Stole ideas.

6. No time for you.

7. Didn't trust you.

8. Talked down.

9. Gave false hopes.

10. Belittled you.

11. Made you feel like an underdog.

12. Took advantage of you.

13. Gave only negative feedback.

14. Set up inconsistent rules.

15. Lied.

16. Would fly off the handle. You lived in fear when he was around.

17. Took on all the responsibilities. You felt like you were unimportant.

18. Used their position to overpower you.

19. Gave no direction. I didn't even know what doing a good job meant.

20. Would say things like, "I must see you in my office after work," I experienced tension throughout the day.

21. Intimidated.

22. Put your ideas down.

23. Keeps laying extra things on you to do and not even being considerate enough to ask for your help or say "Thank you."

24. Negative attitude.

25. Saw you as important only as someone who produced—not as a person.

26. Compared you to other people.

27. Made you feel unwanted—like staff meetings never even looked at you.

28. Smooth talker, but no substance.

29. Never satisfied, nitpicker.

30. Would show you how much he produced when he was in your job before you.

31. Always had to get the last word in.

32. Would make you take his responsibilities, like dealing with tough, angry customers.

33. Would yell at you in front of others. I felt so small!

34. Played favorites.

35. Would socialize with the men, but not the women. It gave men the edge for promotions.

36. Critical facial expressions, heavy eyebrows, etc.

37. Close-minded.

38. You'd bat your brains out working and it was never noticed.

39. Used sarcasm or embarrassment.

40. Assumed I knew what he wanted or what he was thinking.

And, of course, the most interesting response—a manager said, "I just know that Johnny Paycheck sang his song 'Take this job and shove it' while he was employed by my discouraging manager!"

Were any of these responses similar to some of yours? If so, the pattern of the discouraging leader is already forming. See how much you already know about discouragement?

Your Exercise to Identify the Characteristics of Encouraging Leaders

Think of the most Encouraging leader, boss, supervisor, or foreman you have ever experienced. When you identify this person, list at least five characteristics, traits, or "ways of being" that this leader exhibited that encouraged you. Again be global or specific. List below:

_____

_____

_____

_____

_____

Now compare your responses to the responses of other leaders. Question: "What were some of the ingredients or characteristics present in the most Encouraging manager, supervisor, leader, or foreman that you ever experienced?"

1. Listened to you, _really_ listened.
2. Respected your abilities, believed in you.
3. Saw what you did right as well as pointing out what you did wrong.
4. Could delegate responsibility.
5. Enthusiasm.
6. Sense of humor.
7. Admitted mistakes himself.
8. Gave you credit for your ideas.
9. Could recognize when you needed a lift and was there.
10. Interested in you as a person.
11. Was at peace with himself.
12. Consistent rules, in fact, had the staff play a part in developing the rules.
13. Good teacher—willing to share ideas.
14. Criticized constructively.
15. Followed through on promises.
16. Honest, genuine, real.

17. Positive.

18. Permitted freedom and independence as long as you got your job done. You didn't feel smothered or claustrophobic.

19. Gave you a feeling that things you said in confidence would be kept in confidence.

20. Said "Hello," or "Glad to see you" in the morning.

21. I'd hear comments from my manager's boss to me like, "Bob tells me you're doing a great job." What a lift that would give me.

22. Accepted me even if I pointed out how things could be better in the department or if I criticized him.

23. Showed you how what you did was important to the company. It really motivated me to see that my job was significant.

24. Helped me feel like part of the team.

25. Did little things like reassuring me when I came back from vacation that I was missed.

26. I knew exactly what was expected of me.

27. I felt very creative around him. If he didn't like my idea he would give me full credit for it.

28. My first day on the job he took me around to meet everyone and I felt accepted immediately.

29. Fair but firm.

30. Vulnerable and would share his own shortcomings.

31. He would always be available to talk to. Gave you time.

32. Believed in me. I felt special and unique but so did everybody else.

33. Would remember our conversations.

34. Open-minded to new ideas.

35. Non-defensive.

36. Gave good leadership. Could lift the teams' spirits. Saw obstacles as challenges.

37. Was a terrific example. I even quit smoking and started dieting following her example. She was a total person.

38. Professional—never backbiting or putting down people. Even when he was attacked he listened and rationally explained his position.

39. Warm, but not a warmth stemming from weakness.

40. After disciplining you, he gave you hope and a new start.

Do any of your responses match the responses of the other respondents? If so, you are beginning to sense that there is such a person that people agree on as being Encouraging.

It is a person with a certain style. Let's contrast those characteristics given to discouraging people with those characteristics given to encouraging leaders. We can build on these ideas and you can use this as a checklist to look occasionally to keep yourself on the encouraging track (see chart on page 16). Soon, most of the encouraging styles will be a natural part of you.

Ten crucial things to remember:
Ten practical things to do from Chapter 1:

1. Remember: Your leadership style makes the difference in attitude, pride, productivity, trust, involvement, creativity and morale, so
Do: Make a commitment to become an even more encouraging leader by developing and using the skills and attitudes identified as being present in the most effective leaders.

2. Remember: The encouraging leader is not a deep-rooted psychological concept or a mystical theory but is, very simply, a person who carries a "way of being" that tends to lead to a more harmonious and productive relationship with employees, so
Do: Ask yourself these questions that lead to practical, usable answers. 1. What were some of the characteristics or "ways of being" in the most encouraging leader I experienced? 2. How can I employ some of his or her ways of being with my people today?

3. Remember: Discouraging leaders tend to talk too much while encouraging leaders to spend more time listening to their peoples' concerns, frustrations, ideas, pressures and goals, etc., and so
Do: Meet with your most discouraged person and really listen to his or her perspective. After understanding,

A Leader's Checklist of Strategies to Encourage

Tends to Discourage	Neither Discouraging Nor Encouraging	Tends to Encourage
1. I tend to talk too much and not listen enough. (Ch. 3)		I spend a great deal of time listening to my people.
2. My attitude at work has been negative lately. (Chs. 5, 8, 9)		I have a positive, optimistic attitude toward my work and my people.
3. I have been spending more time on what my people do wrong than on what they do correctly. (Ch. 4)		I make a conscious effort to point out the thing that my people do right as well as wrong.
4. I haven't recently shown each of my people why his or her work is important. (Ch. 5)		I believe that each one of my employees knows how meaningful his or her contribution is.
5. I make all of the decisions (Chs. 9, 10)		I involve my people in most of the decisions on how we can most effectively achieve the organization's goals.
6. I think my people would probably say that I am only interested in them as producers, not people. (Ch. 3)		I'm genuinely interested in my peoples' lives and have a good feel of each person's individual long-term goals.

7. I tend to be closed-minded to new ideas or ways of doing things. (Chs. 3, 9, 10)

I am open-minded toward my peoples' ideas.

8. My people rarely bring me new ideas. (Chs. 8, 9, 10)

I can count on new ideas from people daily.

9. My people see me as a perfectionist. (Chs. 3, 9, 10)

When an employee makes a mistake, it is not a catastrophe, so we simply correct it and set up a system so that it minimizes the chance of it happening again.

10. When a new employee arrives I haven't been sensitive to that "anxious first day feeling." I just put the person on the job without any preparation. (Chs. 3, 5)

When a new employee starts, I listen to his or her feelings about the job, provide a safe atmosphere where the person can ask questions and introduce the person to each staff member.

11. When an employee is absent for a period of time or takes a vacation, I just assume that he or she can come back on the job without a welcome. (Ch. 3)

I am sensitive to the feelings a person has when being away from work for a while.

12. I have not been totally genuine with my people at times. (Chs. 6, 7, 9)

I believe that my people trust me.

13. Sometimes my discipline meetings are vague or

When I discipline people, I tell them very specifically why they are

A Leader's Checklist of Strategies to Encourage (continued)

Tends to Discourage	Neither Discouraging Nor Encouraging	Tends to Encourage
sometimes I avoid my responsibilities as a manager who needs to keep people on track. (Ch. 7)		being disciplined, what I specifically expect from them, and I show my belief that they can improve.
14. I tend to feel that I am not the most optimistic person in my department. (Chs. 5, 8)		I am a positive team leader who communicates "We can do it."
15. I play favorites, or make special exceptions for certain people. (Chs. 3, 6, 7)		I try to treat everyone equall.
16. I am not a good model for my people. (Chs. 4, 5, 9)		I feel that if everyone followed my work habits as an example things would be better.
17. I criticize my employees in front of each other. (Chs. 3, 7)		I discipline and confront my discouraged, unproductive people in private.
18. I take on too much, including what should be their responsibilities. (Chs. 4, 6, 10)		I have confidence in my people that with proper training they can do the work. I delegate responsibilities.

19. I lack humor in the office. (Chs. 4, 5, 8)

20. I tend to keep to myself the things I know. (Chs. 4, 9, 10)

21. I feel that I do too much nitpicking and flawfinding. (Chs. 4, 5, 6)

22. I probably take too much credit that could be given to them. (Chs. 5, 9)

23. I just don't give my people enough of my time. (Chs. 3, 9)

24. I tend to use intimidation or pulling rank to motivate my people. (Chs. 3, 4, 9)

25. I emphasize competition amongst my people. (Ch. 10)

26. I recognize only jobs well done. (Chs. 3, 10)

I have worked to create an atmosphere where people can laugh at mistakes.

Everything (except confidential material) that I know I am willing to share with my people.

I am more like a talent scout and have an ability to see hidden assets and resources in my people.

I am constantly trying to give credit where credit is due.

My people know and really feel that I have an open door for them when they need it.

I tend to use encouragement to motivate my people.

I focus on mutual cooperation as opposed to competition to build team power.

I give recognition for effort and improvement, not only the finished task.

19

A Leader's Checklist of Strategies to Encourage (continued)

Tends to Discourage	Neither Discouraging Nor Encouraging	Tends to Encourage
27. I blow up or explode at mistakes. (Chs. 3, 4, 9, 10)		I can deal with things rationally and get the ship back on course.
28. I feel that I am different from my people and am more important than them. (Chs. 3, 5, 6, 9)		I am a team player and everyone has his or her responsibilities

Keep this checklist with you as a reminder to you during times when you observe unmotivated people to help you find ways to lift them.

make a plan based on what you heard. (See Ch. 3 for more intensive details on listening and understanding.)

4. Remember: Discouraging leaders were identified as being those who focused in on what was wrong, rather than what employees did correctly, so
Do: Take a few minutes of your time to think of what your people have done correctly and share it. Don't assume a good job. Give them a lift by letting them know you notice the routine! (See Ch. 4 for further details and positive approaches.)

5. Remember: Discouraging leaders rarely show people why their role is necessary and what contribution it provides, so
Do: Give your peoples' work meaning "beyond the paycheck." Show them how their work is significant. (See Ch. 5 for further details on how to give job meaning.)

6. Remember: Discouraging leaders disrespect people, believing that they are incapable while encouraging managers respect employees by giving them the tough task and conveying a "you can do it" attitude, so
Do: Convey positive expectations in a discouraged person by giving him or her a job that you might ordinarily not because of feelings that the person couldn't handle it. (See Ch. 6 for further details on how to build confidence in your people.)

7. Remember: Discouraging leaders often use public embarrassment, sarcasm, or cynicism to deal with difficult employees while encouraging leaders know how to constructively steer the difficult employee back on the path, so
Do: Memorize and use the 10 Step Process of Assertive Encouragement listed in Ch. 7 if you need to discipline an employee.

8. Remember: Discouraging leaders use the styles of making excuses, blaming others or acting pessimistic during tough times while the encouraging managers face the crises head-on with an optimistic solution seeking attitude, so
Do: If you are facing a crisis at this moment show your organization what you are made of, and be a positive

example to your people by 1. facing the challenge directly and 2. getting your people to find solutions. (For further information see Ch. 8.)

9. Remember: Discouraging leaders have weak egos and thus use their job to fill their egos while encouraging leaders use their energies to reach the goals instead, so **Do:** If your ego is in conflict with another person or your supervisor, or with the achievement of any organizational goal, put your priorities in order and ask yourself, "Would I rather look good or achieve success?" (For further details see Ch. 9.)

10. Remember: Discouraging leaders tend to emphasize competition amongst the employees while encouraging managers instead highlight the necessity for cooperation to build Team Power. (For further details on how to develop Team Power, see Ch. 10.)

Now, begin your leadership self-development program. Learn how to encourage your unproductive or unmotivated people by having the insights to understand them for what they really are, discouraged.

Insights to Make You
a Motivating Leader

Motivating leaders have a powerful ally. They have no less than human nature on their side. Yes, the most natural behavior in the world is the infant's high levels of motivation to explore—at nature's pace—their world. The infant doesn't panic after making a mistake, but simply looks to correct it. However, when the infant experiences criticisms of his or her imperfect tries, feelings of personal inadequacies in this superior world develop. Anticipation of possible mistakes activate the little one to seek caution. The original natural motivation to create and explore becomes bridled by fear. Discouragement sets in. (Years later in the organization we see this unmotivated person as afraid to try new ways of doing things, or as a perfectionist, or sometimes as migraine-oriented or as having a poor self-concept.) But human nature started out on the infant's side.

It's human nature as well for the infant to want to contribute, to share what he or she can give. Thousands of pictures can flash through one's head of a child proudly holding out a personal drawing or picking a flower to give to Grandma. (While lecturing at a university in Vancouver B.C., I asked 500 people to draw a picture of a horse and requested that a few volunteers share their drawing with the group. I had only two takers—one, a four-year-old girl, the other, a five-year-old boy—the two

23

children in the audience!) Why were there no adults? The child's desire to contribute gets blocked when he or she runs into superior know-it-alls, critics, and again, perfectionists. In the organization we see this unmotivated individual as one who never gives anything extra—never wants to contribute, or one who shared an idea before and it was stolen by someone else who took credit. But remember, originally human nature did not design this being that way.

It's human nature as well for the infant to want to belong to a social unit. Infants respond when people walk into their room. They enjoy being picked up, always want to be included in everyone's plans and proudly say to strangers, "That's my Daddy." It's only after they experience "conditional belonging" (we accept you only if you act in this or that fashion) that they feel partial belonging, part-time worth. (In organizations we see this person as the outsider, the rebel, the one who just won't listen and cooperate!)

And it's human nature for the infant to be open, honest, genuine and vulnerable. The golden realness starts to bronze upon hearing the warnings issued about life. "Don't talk to those people," "It's a dog-eat-dog world," "You can't trust . . .," and "If people are nice to you it's only because they want something from you," are just a few of the many insights that create the hard callousness we see in some adults. (In the organization we see them as closed-minded to our ideas, paranoid, distrustful, cold and at a distance.) But remember, they weren't born that way.

The infant has a high level of motivation to grow, to explore, to be more, to contribute, to belong and to be open, honest, genuine and vulnerable. Sometimes life's experiences dicourage them, but an encouraging leader—with help from an ally, human nature, can now remove the chains blocking the natural motivation and help people find fulfillment.

To encourage, the leader needs a model or a map of what makes people tick. The map used in this book was first drawn up by psychiatrist Alfred Adler and later detailed by his student Rudolf Dreikurs. Adler's map was selected because it has two very important elements.

First, the common sense psychiatrist was very practical and interested only in workable ideas. Secondly, this map is based on positive techniques to motivate. The emphasis of positive over negative is obvious when we look back on the list in Ch. 1 on behaviors that "worked" to motivate. This map of understanding human behavior has five major insights, many outlined by Adler and a few added from *Turning People On, How to be an Encouraging Person.* (Prentice-Hall, 1977)

An encouraging leader's insights into people

Insight 1: People act out of the way they (not I) look at life. To motivate them I have to spend some time understanding their "private logic."

Insight 2: People can best be understood by observing the social consequences of their actions.

Insight 3: Individual uniquenesses are not to be ignored, but rather are to be explored and highlighted. Uniquenesses are the very source of personal energy.

Insight 4: Unmotivated individuals are not sick, bad, lazy, or stupid. Unmotivated individuals are discouraged. The antidote to discouragement is encouragement.

Insight 5: People are viewed as being responsible for their actions.

Encouraging Insight 1

The four-year-old boy with a tykish curiosity on his face nudges his mother as he looks up to her and asks the simple question, "Mommy, where's Daddy?"

Mother looks down and casually responds, "Honey, your father is tied up at the office."

Envisioning his poor Daddy gagging and in ropes on the office floor and his mother so unconcerned, the little boy panics.

He acts out of the way he (not mother) looks at life. The philosophy of phenomenology argues that our behaviors stem from our view of the situation, not the "facts" of the situation. The facts are that the little boy's father is OK. His panic is a result of his subjective view.

Epictetus, the stoic philosopher, concluded, "Men are not disturbed by things, only thinking makes them disturbed." Indeed, Adler argued that "if a person believes he or she was just bitten by a snake it matters not whether the bite actually took place from a strictly psychological perspective." This person's behavior will be determined by that view. To take another example, it is insignificant as to whether people are really following or not following the "paranoid" person to kill him. The person's behavior will be dictated by the view, "they are after me." He will be frightened of what amounts to, in fact, no one. An encouraging leader starts with the other person's phenomenological view, the "private logic."

One member of a church never volunteered to help out at the fund raising bazaars. The pastor was concerned since some parishioners felt she was taking advantage of everyone else's work. The church leader decided to talk with the troubled member of the church. In the conversation the pastor discovered that the last two suggestions the so-called lazy lady made at a meeting about how to improve the bazaar were flatly rejected.

She apologetically shared—"I felt put down and stupid, and that I really had nothing to offer anyway. I thought that they'd be happy if I didn't get in the way." The leader shared this with the group (with the woman's permission) and the following year she was selected to be a contributing member of the baked goods committee— all because the leader took the time to understand the "private logic" of his church citizen. She acted out of the way she (not the congregation) looked at things.

The simplest, yet at the same time one of the most incomprehensible rules of human behavior is that all behavior makes sense when we see it from the actor's perspective; the four-year-old who panicked at Dad being tied up and the uninvolved church member's "irresponsibility" made total sense when we began seeing it from their view. And so does the rebel's behavior, the change resistor, the chronic absentee, the alcoholic, and even the suicidal person's behavior make sense when we explore their private logic, and their limited vantage point. The behavior may not make sense to the observer, who has another "private logic," but it makes sense to the actor.

With this awareness of insight# 1 (people act out of the way they, not I, look at life), what would an encouraging leader do that someone lacking the insight wouldn't? Consider these two directions that a leader could take with a person who is slowly becoming unmotivated. One way is to move "away from" understanding the person's private logic—the other is to "move toward" understanding the person's private logic.

The discouraging leader	The encouraging leader
Moving away from Actor's logic (or imposing one's own logic on the person).	Moving toward understanding private logic of the other.
"You'll just never get anywhere in the organization if you keep associating with those negative people and listening to their ideas."	"Your friends and I often disagree about things. And I'd really be interested in better understanding what they feel is wrong here. Their suggestions and yours could be helpful to make the organization grow. But it will be helpful only if we can talk. Can you share some of your thoughts with me?"

Which will be a more effective leadership approach— the one that moves away, ignores, or squelches a different private logic, or the one that moves toward understanding the joining of two private logics to form a "common sense?"

It is important to keep in mind that moving toward another private logic does not necessarily mean moving toward agreeing with their phenomenological world. You can truly understand their world, but disagree with it from your world. But, of course, there will be times when the "private logic" of another begins to make sense to you. What a benefit to gain! An increased insight is yours because of your willingness to understand.

Every day provides free opportunities to sharpen your leadership skills by mastering the first insight of encouragement: People act out of the way they (Not I) look at life. Try it with someone who you totally disagree with. Begin to see how they think. Discovering how another thinks is a secret to success with others. Captain Lou Puskas, one of the top fishermen in the Eastern United States, when asked why he is so successful in pulling in the big catch responded, "You've got to think like a fish. When it rains or when it is windy, calm, sunny, you imagine where they would go. Then you go there."

Whether you are a fisher of men, a vice-president of a steel company, or the manager of a record shop, understanding how your people think will be the key to your success with them.

Encouraging Insight 2

The manager of a small card shop becomes furious and loses her temper after learning that her employees had been rude to some customers. She starts kicking card racks and shouting obscenities to them. The two employees decide to walk out on her—leaving no one else in the shop to observe her actions. How long do you think she continued kicking and throwing? Not long. Why? No audience, no show! No one to observe, so the behavior no longer has a social consequence, that is, the reactions of others.

Did you ever spot a young child fall off a bicycle and look around to see if anyone was there before he or she decided to cry or not? Did you ever see someone at work being complimented with a statement like, "You look super in blue?" What did you observe about this person's future dress patterns? Were you ever told by another person you respected that you had a real talent at something or other? Did you not highlight that particular asset or talent in that other person's presence? People's behavior can best be understood by being aware of their "private logic" of what other people are looking for in them.

Now, the interesting fact about people is that the social consequences of attention and recognition are so important that many conclude, "If I can't get my attention needs taken care of by doing the right thing I will do the *wrong* thing (discouraged). But at least the social consequences of attention are received."

Here is one example of how misdirected behavior to get attention was rerouted by an encouraging leader by altering the social consequences: An 18-year-old working at a fast-food restaurant was an extreme attention-getter in the presence of the other workers and customers, and would even "act out" when the manager was in the room. The manager wanted to do everything to help her before firing her and he told her so. Yet, the teenager continued her loud-mouth behavior. In a discussion during her final warning the manager found that the girl had an older sister who did everything perfectly, who was straight "A" in school and who was accepted into one of the most prestigious colleges. The manager also discovered that her attention-seeking girl was always second best and never did get attention from her parents like her sister ... until she got into trouble. Then they noticed her. The insightful manager realized that she didn't give much attention to the girl when she did the right thing, only when she needed discipline. During the next three days the manager would from time to time give her attention for working well with the others. She caught her in the act of "being responsible." The manager created a social setting for the girl to get her attention needs fulfilled through constructive behavior. Her job was saved.

The Encouraging Leader is always aware that people's behavior can best be understood by observing the social consequences of their behavior. The leader tries to understand the person's logic toward "what behavior will work to get me attention!!" When the person's attention needs are fulfilled by positive actions the person becomes increasingly involved and productive.

Dr. Richard Cahn, superintendent of a large northeastern U. S. school district, employs encouragement in the school organization. Cahn concludes about people:

> *It has been my observation that people are more fulfilled by performing well than by performing poorly, by contributing instead of being uncooperative and by feeling recognized rather than by feeling insignificant.*

People can find this fulfillment when an encouraging atmosphere exists. (Dinkmeyer & Losoncy, 1980)

A discouraging leader's approach to a discouraged person	*An encouraging leader's approach to a discouraged person*
I'll wait for that irresponsible behavior to occur again and I will come down on (give my attention) to him or her.	Let me give attention today to what that person does right. If the discouraged behavior occurs again as best as possible I will ignore it. (Not give attention to).
	However, I must immediately give my attention when the person again acts inappropriately.
	Only if the disruptive actions continue will I confront. (See Ch. 7)

Consider the behavior and goals of discouraged people and some alternate encouraging leadership approaches in chart on the following page.

Encouraging Insight 3

In the age of technology society tried to organize individuals into either "this category" or "that category." This was done so people would fit into the finite mind of the computer, limited in its ability to give a person every

Behaviors and Goals of Discouraged People

Behavior	Possible Goal of Behavior	Typical Reaction of Others	Alternate, More Encouraging Approach
Attention-seeking	Attention Feel important when noticed	Reprimand Punishment "Giving in" Name-calling	Ignore Give attention for more appropriate behaviors. Leave the situation (if the audience leaves, the show ends).
Avoidance of responsibility	No pressure No fear of failure Safety Predictability	Name-calling (lazy). Taking responsibility for the discouraged person.	Encourage responsible behaviors No help with responsibility
Lack of confidence	Safety Retreat from reality Pity	Sympathy Pity Blame	Encourage effort Support
Thoughts of worthlessness	Attention Pity Praise-seeking	Praise Pity Blame	Show how worth isn't dependent upon performance but on existence.
Avoidance of competition	No losses Not noticed, singled out, or put on the spot.	Giving "special treatment"	Emphasis on trying—not winning. Communication of idea that a loss is only a suggestion that there is an alternative way of handling a problem.

Behaviors and Goals of Discouraged People (continued)

Behavior	Possible Goal of Behavior	Typical Reaction of Others	Alternate, More Encouraging Approach
Need for power and control	Domination Security-seeking in being boss Reaction against weakness, Inferiority Get own way	Anger "Giving-in" Name-calling	Ignore inappropriate behaviors Try to give attention for cooperative behaviors Refuse to debate
Seeking revenge	Attention Retaliation Control Hurt	Hurt Giving in Fighting Name-calling (no-good person)	Ignore when possible Point out the results of revenge Provide more desirable alternatives
Need for perfection	Success in limited area Predictability Security	Impatience Reward for success	Encourage risks, new experiences Support when things don't go well Emphasize effort
Dishonesty	Escape from punishment Enhance self Escape inferiority Punishment of a rival	Punishment Name-calling Punishing others Blaming	Emphasize truth, not punishment Point out lie in supportive way Ignore tattling
Closed-mindedness	No confusion over values Predictability Avoidance of personal responsibility	Agreement No pressure	Encourage new experiences Help the discouraged person view openness with pride

uniqueness that was rightfully his or hers. But whenever we attempt to "quantify" people, we disqualify their uniqueness. This is unfortunate, and of course, new ways of viewing people to incorporate both the machine and the person at higher levels is inevitable.

That higher level incorporation of machine and person has been described in John Naisbitt's bestseller *Megatrends*. In describing the ten trends society is experiencing, the author calls our age one that needs to provide high technology/high touch. Naisbitt argues that with increased technology must come increased literal and figurative touch of people to fulfill their human needs.

An Encouraging Leader must "touch" people in some way and the touch must be real. How do I know if I'm being touched in a genuine way? I know it if you recognize my uniquenesses, the ways that belong to this special organism called "me."

The Encouraging Leader makes extra-ordinary people out of ordinary ones by showing them that he or she took the time to observe their own unique "private logic," and their own unique talents and goals. The Encouraging Leader may be the first person ever to give them that gift of being felt and understood.

A discouraging leader looks at a group	*An encouraging leader looks at uniquenesses of each member*
"You people . . . ."	"Each of you has something special to offer. Think of what you can contribute in your own unique way."

Encouraging Insight 4

How many people would not want to see faces light up because of their arrival when they walk into a room? How many would not want to feel like they had at least a little rippling effect on the waters of life during their lifetime?

Who would rather be imprisoned in life's possibilities than fully living them? Very few.

Encouraging leaders have human nature on their sides. But discouraged people feel they can't make it, they have nothing to offer, they will make a mistake, they will be taken advantage of, they will be snubbed or laughed at, or they believe there is an "easier way" to fame and success (defined from their own private logic).

It is amazing to see a "lazy person" moved into a new setting with an encouraging leader who recognizes talents, strength, and resources in the person. The laziness somehow or another goes away!

It is incredible to see a "sick" person in the presence of two different psychiatrists—one who talks disease, the other who talks potential. The person walks out of each office differently.

It is awesome to see a "retarded" student in the presence of two different teachers—one who goes with the category of retarded and one who sees the uniqueness of the discouraged youth. The difference is *everything*.

Encouraging Insight 5

The old debate that centered on the issue of what causes human behavior, heredity or environment, seems to be leading to the conclusion that neither is the ultimate influence. A reading of Marilyn Ferguson's extensive work *The Aquarian Conspiracy* provides strong support for a third cause. This newer, more optimistic perspective of what makes people tick argues for the power of self-determination. Adler and many others observed humans who transcended environments devoid of golden spoons to achieve greatness. Adler argued:

> *Do not forget the most important fact that not heredity and not environment are determining factors. Both are giving only the frame and the influence which are answered by the individual in regard to his styled, creative power.*

> Ansbacer and Ansbacer 1956

David Schwartz, in his powerful offering *The Magic of Getting What You Want*, provided some valuable insights into the rewards of self-determinism:

> *Huge, prosperous businesses such as McDonalds, Ford, Kentucky Fried Chicken and Amway were started by people with very little capital. Furthermore, Presidents Coolidge, Hoover, Truman, Eisenhower, Johnson, Nixon, Ford, Carter and Reagan—all except two of the people who led the nation in modern times—were born to poor or modestly well-off parents. Presidents Roosevelt and Kennedy were the only exceptions.*
>
> Schwartz 1983

There are two major perspectives leaders can take toward their people: passive and active. The passive position is one in which the leader sees his or her people with limited capabilities based on factors like environment, circumstances, luck, intelligence, or education. Taking the passive posture often means spending energies digging up the "excuse," the "blame," or the reason for the limitations.

Describing the passive view, I wrote in *You Can Do It*:

> *The unproductive way of understanding the causes for your feelings, thoughts, and actions is to conclude they were caused by someone or something other than yourself. At least four different types of blame receivers can be distinguished. These four are group blame, (The other school is much bigger than ours so they'll beat us); other person blame (e.g., my teachers didn't explain things well); thing blame (e.g., This cloudy weather makes me lazy) and self-blame (e.g., I'm not the kind of person who was built to be a leader).*
>
> Losoncy 1980

Passive leaders wait for circumstances to change, for the right moment to arrive. But waiting for the world to change before we change is like looking into a mirror at our reflection and saying, "You move first."

Active self-starting leaders take responsibility to

make things happen. They take any circumstance, no matter how challenging and say, "It's up to me to mobilize my people resources and find a solution to the problem." Let's contrast the attitudes of two leaders, one passive and one active, and decide which one you would want on your team.

Passive leader outlook	*Active leader outlook*
1. What's the use! I can't control the economy. Only money motivates people and so I'll just have to wait until the economy shifts and my people get their raises before I can expect to see motivated employees.	1. The major reason why most of my employees work is financial and right now the economy is bad. Unfortunately I can't control the world's economy, but, as a leader, I can control many other factors that contribute to productivity, for instance, pride in achievement, recognition for skills and talents, understanding of employee frustration, etc. Let me develop an employee motivation strategy.
2. These kids just aren't motivated. There's nothing I can do about it. It's the schools, the permissive child rearing practices, the increased drug usage, and so on, that causes it. No, there's nothing I can do about the fact that kids nowadays don't want to work.	2. These kids today are an exciting challenge for a manager because some of them are not motivated in the same ways we managers are. Like a detective, I'll spend time learning the clues to solve the problem of motivating the young workers of today. By developing different

strategies, I will be enhancing my skills in motivating an important segment of the work force. Every day of work is a free opportunity for me to understand how to motivate young people; a greater opportunity than to take all of the college courses in the world on motivating people.

3. We tried selling the Smith account before. They are just too stubborn. Don't waste your time!

3. The Smith account is a big one. We want it. The approaches we used before didn't work. Let's brainstorm and find a way!

Which leader will more likely get things done? Obviously the one who tries, the one who believes, "It's up to us to take responsibility and find a solution to the challenge."

Encouraging leaders have respect for the abilities of responsible self-starters. They always do better. And their belief in people motivates their people to soar higher.

Five Insights to Make You a Motivating Leader

People are attracted to the positive energies of a motivating leader. They want a reason to go on, they want to contribute, belong, and be open and genuine. Human nature is on the side of the Motivating Leader.

But, many unmotivated or irresponsible people are discouraged. To encourage it is necessary to have a map of what makes people tick, why they act the way they do.

In this chapter, five insights about people were discussed to better understand them.

Encouraging insight 1: People act out of the way they (not I) look at life. To motivate them I have to spend some time trying to understand their private logic.

Encouraging insight 2: People can best be understood by observing the social consequences of their actions.

Encouraging insight 3: Individual uniquenesses are not to be ignored, but rather explored, even highlighted. Uniquenesses are the very source of personal energies.

Encouraging insight 4: Unmotivated individuals are not sick, bad, lazy or stupid. Unmotivated people are discouraged. The antidote to discouragement is encouragement.

Encouraging insight 5: People are viewed as being responsible for their actions.

Ten Things to Remember
Ten Practical Things to Do from Chapter 2

1. Remember: People operate out of the way they look at life, so
Do: Take some time looking at the world out of the perspective of the discouraged person to sense the private logic. You then will be in a much better position to motivate.

2. Remember: All behavior makes sense when we see it from the actor's perspective, so
Do: Instead of condemning another's actions, first understand that the behavior was logical at the time. Communicate that understanding, then add a new perspective to help the person grow.

3. Remember: People can best be understood by observing the social consequences of their actions, so
Do: Discouraged, unmotivated, irresponsible people need to receive different social consequences from you, the leader. Don't give attention for negative behaviors, but recognize the positive behavior.

4. Remember: Contrary to the ideas of the past, it is now realized that, for the good of the whole department, emphasizing competition hurts more than helps, so
Do: Carefully assess your everyday style to eliminate any

attitudes that you might be conveying that play one person against the other. (See Ch. 10 for further details.)

5. Remember: Your unproductive, unmotivated, or uninvolved employees are discouraged and may be telling you that they feel as though they don't belong or maybe that their contribution is insignificant, so
Do: Make a plan to help your discouraged person feel a part of the team. (See Ch. 10) and feel that the work he or she does each day has meaning. (See Ch. 5.)

6. Remember: A few of your unmotivated people may feel lost, alienated, or just like another producer without uniqueness, so
Do: If you sense that an employee has developed the feeling "I am just a number, not a person," become determined to give a few extra minutes to fire up his or her feelings of uniqueness.

7. Remember: Most people are more fulfilled by performing well than performing poorly, by contributing than by being uncooperative, and by feeling recognized than by feeling insignificant. People can find this fulfillment in an encouraging atmosphere, so
Do: With this attitude in mind proceed to develop the hundreds of skills, strategies, and attitudes that encouraging managers have.

8. Remember: Individual uniquenesses are not to be ignored, but rather explored and highlighted, so
Do: Identify unique skills, talents, strengths, and resources in each one of your people—Tell them!

9. Remember: Unmotivated individuals are not sick, bad, lazy, or stupid. They are discouraged, so
Do: The remedy to discouragement is not blaming, diagnosing, or name calling. The remedy to discouragement is your encouragement. Reread the chart on pp. 31 and encourage!!

10. Remember: Active managers believe that people can be responsible to solve problems, so
Do: Communicate to your people the belief that you believe in them and instead of looking for excuses together, look for answers together.

It's now time to get to the skills development program of the book. Keep in mind the power present in the "way of being" of the leader and the five insights about people. Chapter 3 addresses techniques that you can use today to bring about better communication, more harmony, and mutual respect into your unit.

Positive Leadership Approaches to Resolve Differences

Ironically, leaders are the most dependent people in the organization. The higher one is the more people he or she needs to hold them up. Leaders are dependent upon those they lead. Leaders' successes are based on the performance of those they lead. When the followers are motivated to work together to achieve the membership's goals, the leaders become successful. When, however, the members of the organization are immersed in conflict, miscommunication, or misunderstanding, a different type of motivation exists—a negative motivation. A negative motivation is seen in a selfish narrow-mindedness, a desire to prove someone wrong, and a feeling of personal martyrdom. These misdirected motivations waste energies that could be used constructively instead of in destructive directions. Both the organization and the leader lose.

By default, the leader is the most likely candidate to take the responsibility to initiate plans to resolve the differences, amongst people. The leader has the most to lose. Differences result from what in Chapter 2 was referred to as the "private logic" held by each member. Leadership's task, is to bring together the private logic of many to form a common sense.

But even the most highly motivated leader is cognizant of the fact that resolving differences of private logic is no easy goal. The task is formidable—especially when you consider the natural disagreements that occur.

The private logic of the commissioned sales person is often so different from the private logic of the collection department.

The private logic of the waitress (who faces the public and hears food complaints) is almost always different from the private logic of the chef who cooked the food.

The private logic of the beauty salon owner who invested thousands of dollars to start the business is often different from the private logic of the haircutter employed there who wonders why "I only get fifty percent and the owner gets fifty percent."

The private logic of the high school football coach is different from the private logic of the players' parents sitting on the bench.

In bigger organizations the private logic of individuals snowballs into a "limited group logic" that makes the issue even more complex to address. One of the most interesting experiences I ever faced was serving as a consultant to one of Pennsylvania's school districts. In this capacity, I had the opportunity to work with school board members, school administrators, teachers, custodians, students, and parents. I worked with each group on "How to Be Encouraging" and "How to Communicate More Effectively." The length of the sessions varied from three to thirty hours with each group.

What insights I gained! Every, yes, every group in the organization had something in common. Each thought he or she was getting the "raw deal" in the organization. The board members, for example, felt they were the "unpaid scapegoats" and were basically unappreciated. The school administrators felt that they had their hands tied and couldn't make any decisions or else the boat would rock. If they did, the axe would come down on them. The teachers blamed the school board for not caring, the administrators for not disciplining the students, and the children for not listening. The secondary teachers even blamed the elementary teachers for not preparing the children for high school. In turn, the elementary teachers blamed the parents for permissive child-rearing practices. The custodians criticized the administrators for not laying the law down on cleanliness in the cafeteria and hallways. The janitors blamed the teachers and students for not "picking up" in the classes. The students blamed the administrators for tough, inflexible rules and accused many teachers of not caring and of being interested only in getting their paychecks. The parents blamed the school board members for using their positions as stepping stones to gain political clout. The parents blamed the administrators for punishing their children when the teachers were at fault. And the parents also blamed the teachers for not teaching!

In other experiences, I found these misunderstandings to exist in most organizations. Unfortunately, the energy being used to build stronger arguments in support of one's own private logic or the limited group logic could be energies diverted to achieving common goals.

This chapter lists approaches to building understanding, mutual respect, and open communication amongst your people. If your unit is faced with any of these problems, this chapter has relevance:

1. Social cliques
2. Interdepartmental conflicts
3. Scapegoats
4. Unappreciated people
5. Stubbornness
6. Poor morale
7. Lack of communication
8. Disrespect
9. Misunderstandings
10. Egoism

Six approaches to resolving
people problems

1. Transferring
2. Un-diagnosing
3. Peeking

4. De-escalating

5. Exposing

6. Linking

1. Transferring

Transferring is a leadership approach taken to minimize jealousies, narrow-mindedness, misunderstandings, and differences based on differing responsibilities. Transferring is most appropriately used when some sort of disharmony exists amongst people or departments. It is an attempt to broaden the "private logic" of the parties and to create a common sense. Transferring is based on Encouraging Insight #1 from Ch. 2: People operate out of the way they (not I) look at life. To motivate them I have to spend some time trying to understand their private logic.

The charismatic vice-president of Human Resources was continually confronted by the vice-president of Finance about the irresponsible sales department. The accounting executive would explode, "Our psychopathic sales force promises everything and wants to give away the world to the customer. All you have to do is to be a sharp-talking worm brain to be a salesperson. They have no responsibilities but to make a sale at any cost and then we in finance face the burden of accounting for the monies in the end."

The Human Resources specialist was intrigued because he was continually bombarded by the vice-president of Sales reflecting frustration over the money man always on his back.

Is there an answer? Yes—Transferring. The vice-president urged both leaders to take three days and get into the work world of the other—to transfer themselves to the other's world and see what life looks like. They were encouraged to open their minds, feel the unique pressures and frustration of the "other side," and then communicate to develop a practical plan to work together.

The vice-president of Finance made this report to his people a month later:

The pressures on our sales people here are different than the pressures on us. First, they feel the responsibility from the whole company to produce, produce, produce. And it's tough during these times. Secondly, they get to know the customer intimately and sometimes they make promises based on the personal relationship. In accounting perhaps the customer is viewed more as an account, maybe more objectively, and we have trouble understanding their pressures of that specific account. Thirdly, the salesperson's living and in fact, retention of his or her job is based simply on sales. Our jobs aren't. I guess if I were in sales maybe some of my attitudes about salespeople would change and would be more in harmony with their views. I have tried to understand their world and they have tried to understand our pressures. Together we are developing a plan to make life easier for everyone.

Transferring involves encouraging people to spend some time in the world of responsibilities of the other. For example, the grill person at the fast-food restaurant should work up front for a day and the order taker should work behind the grill.

How many ways can you, as a leader, think of using Transferring to help your organization?

_____

_____

_____

2. Undiagnosing

Sometimes leaders have been able to put their fingers on a problem, diagnose, and even label the problem but have no practical course of action to follow to motivate. The diagnosis didn't work, so the next logical course of action is to ... undiagnose.

Ben was a troubled employee who everyone knew had drinking problems. And while it was interfering with his performance only slightly, the potential for poor work quality existed in the future. Ben's manager, Ed, labeled Ben an alcoholic and this was generally supported by the personnel people. The well-intentioned manager even suggested Ben seek help but Ben kept resisting, saying that everything would be OK.

Ed realized that having a label "alcoholic" did nothing in itself to help Ben unless Ben was motivated to go for assistance. With a strong desire to help the discouraged person he decided to do something that might be more practical.

First, Ed forgot about the label of alcoholic (undiagnose). Next, he transferred to Ben's world to see how his situation looked from his own "private logic" (see Ch. 2). While taking a few minutes sitting in his office he took a mental trip to Ben's world.

Diagnosing	*Undiagnosing and transferring*
CONCLUSION: Ben is alcoholic	CONCLUSION: "My life is in shambles. My wife left me, took my daughter with her. And it's all my fault. On top of that I'm deadened on my job with no promotion possible. And work is terribly routine, boring and gives me no satisfaction. I've gained so much weight recently it's uncomfortable for me to even walk. I've lost respect for myself. Life seems to be hopeless and I'm digging myself into a deeper and deeper rut. Nothing seems to matter anymore. The only time I feel good about things is when I get away and get a few belts of whiskey. The bartender and the guys at the club understand me. They remember my high school touchdown."

After experiencing the Transfer, Ed was in a much better position to understand and connect to Ben's world. By accurately understanding Ben, Ed could apply some of the strategies of encouragement. He decided that in a small way he could promise some of that valuable social attention that the bartender gave to Ben. So he started talking to Ben about his sports experiences and was able to apply some of the assets involved in being a football player on a team to Ben's role at work. All I can say is that Ed said, "Ben's face lit up."

TREATMENT: Recommend he seeks help	TREATMENT:
	1. Share with Ben his assets that you admire.
	2. Discuss with him his feelings about alternate future possibilities.
	3. Convey an understanding of the difficulties that he must be experiencing at this time.
	4. Convey *hope* and open the door to future communication.
BEN'S RESPONSE: No	BEN'S RESPONSE: Feelings of importance and acceptance, more willing to communicate. With this increased willingness to talk with someone who respected him it enhanced the chance of accepting advice.

Undiagnosing is the process of unlabeling someone (lazy, paranoid, etc.) after discovering that the label gave no practical help. And instead transferring to the person's world to see what it looks like, spot the needs, the pressures, and frustrations, and move to remediate the problem.

How could you use undiagnosing in your organization as a more effective leader?

_____

_____

3. Peeking

Peeking is an approach that many motivating leaders use quite naturally. Yet the same ideas are available to any sensitive person who wants to peek beyond the surface of someone's actions or feelings and see the "real self." Peeking is consistent with psychiatrist Carl Jung's concept that what we see in people is often their mask and not their real self. Jung argued that many times, the mask may even be the exact opposite of the real underlying self. This poem expresses the difference between the real and underlying selves and gets one "in tune" with the importance of peeking at discouraged people.

Please Hear What I Am Not Saying

> Don't be fooled by me
> Don't be fooled by the face I wear.
>> For I wear a Mask. I wear a thousand masks,
>> Masks that I'm afraid to take off.
>> And none of them are me.
> Pretending is an art that's second nature with me,
>> But don't be fooled,
>> For god's sake don't be fooled.
> I give you the impression that I'm secure.
>> That all is sunny and unruffled with me,
>> Within as well as without.
>> That confidence is my name and coolness my game
>> That water's calm and I'm in command,
>> And that I need no one.
> But don't believe me,
> Please,

My surface may seem smooth, but my surface is my
    mask,
    My every-varying and ever-concealing mask,
    Beneath lies no smugness, no complacence.
    Beneath dwells the real me in confusion, in fear,
    In aloneness.
But I hide this
I don't want anybody to know it.
I panic at the thought of my weakness and fear being
    exposed
That's why I frantically create a mask to hide behind.
    A nonchalant, sophisticated facade, to help me
    pretend
    to shield me from the glance that knows.
But such a glance is precisely my salvation,
My salvation, and I know it.
That is, if it's followed by acceptance. If it's followed
    by love.
It's the only thing that can liberate me from myself,
    From my own self-built prison walls,
    From the barriers that I so painstakingly erect.
It's the only thing that will assure me of what I can
    assure myself,
    That I am really worth something.
But I don't tell you this, I don't dare.
I'm afraid to.
I'm afraid your glance will not be followed by
    acceptance and love.
I'm afraid that deep down I'm nothing,
    That I'm no good,
    And that you will see this and reject me,
So I play my game,
    My desperate pretending game,
    With a facade of masks,
    That glittering but empty parades of masks.
    And my life becomes a front.
I idly chatter to you in the suave tones of surface talk.
I tell you everything that's really nothing,
    And nothing of what's everything,
    Of what's crying within me.
So when I'm through my routine—
    Don't be fooled by what I'm saying.
Please listen carefully, and hear what I'm Not saying.
    What I'd like to be able to say,
    What for survival I need to say,
    But what I can't say,

49

I dislike hiding.
Honestly.
I dislike the superficial game I'm playing,
    The superficial, phoney game.
I really like to be genuine and spontaneous,
    And me, but you've got to help me
You've got to hold out your hand,
    Even when that's the last thing I seem to want, or
    need.
Only you can wipe away from my eyes the blank stare
    of the
    breathing dead.
    Only you can call me into aliveness.
Each time you're kind, and gentle, and encouraging,
    Each time you try to understand because you
    really care,
    My heart begins to grow wings, very small wings,
        Very feeble wings.
        But wings.
With your sensitivity and sympathy
    And your power of understanding,
    You can breathe life into me.
I want you to know that.
I want you to know how important you are to me.
    How you can be a creator of the person that is me,
    If you choose to,
    Please choose to.
You alone can break down the wall behind which I
    tremble,
You alone can remove my mask,
You alone can release me from my shadow-world of
    panic and uncertainty,
    From my lonely prison.
So do not pass me by.
Please, do not pass me by.
It will not be easy for you,
A long conviction of worthlessness builds strong walls.
The nearer you approach to me, the blinder I may
    strike back.
It's irrational, but despite what the books say about
    man,
    I am irrational.
I fight against the very thing I cry out for.
But I am told that love is stronger than strong walls,
    And in this lies my hope.
My only hope.

Please try to beat down those walls with firm hands.
    But with gentle hands.
Who am I, you may wonder?
I am someone you know very well.
For I am every man and woman you meet.

Anonymous

Jack and Judy sold household products in their family business and built up a few hundred other family businesses who did the same. The husband and wife were known for their sensitivity to wedding anniversaries and would always do something nice for their people. On one occasion they forgot an important anniversary and the couple, the Harris's, became upset. John Harris angrily asserted, "You know, we've been with you much longer than most, and others—even on their first anniversary—are honored."

Judy, a sensitive lady, saw his surface emotion of anger. But she didn't respond to the anger and instead peeked at the real underlying feeling, hurt.

"John, what a horrible oversight on our part. I'm sure it must hurt you and Sally after how hard you worked this year. I guess at times Jack and I get caught up in our work and we make mistakes. We hope that our oversight isn't viewed as a lack of caring or respect but simply an oversight. It won't happen again."

Imagine how a different ending could have resulted if Judy responded to the surface emotion of anger rather than hurt!

Peeking is looking beyond any emotion or behavior and asking "what might really be at the roots?" and responding to the underlying emotion.

- Could anger really be hurt?
- Could acting overconfident be lack of confidence?
- Could acting disinterested be afraid of getting involved?
- Could "I'm happy just the way things are now" be "I'm afraid of taking a risk and failing"?
- Could "I hate you" be "I love you"?
- Could "I don't care" be "I care too much and it hurts and I must numb myself"?

51

- Could "sarcasm" be the hard crust on a very sensitive person?

- Could "no soliciting" mean "If you get to me I know I'll buy so I need signs to keep you away"?

- Could "I'm busy tonight" mean "I'm not—but I can't let you know that I have nothing to do"?

Identify some ways you could use peeking to become a more sensitive and effective leader in your organization.

_____

_____

_____

_____

4. De-escalating

De-escalation is a concept based on the writings and ideas of Carl R. Rogers, the psychologist who shook the world with insights in the 60s that have now become a way of life in effective communications.

Rogers argues that there are two major ways of taking in the words of another. One way is to judge, the other way is to make every attempt to understand. In *On Becoming a Person*, Rogers wrote:

> ... the major barrier to mutual interpersonal communication is our very natural tendency to judge, to evaluate, to approve or disapprove, the statements of the other person or group ... Although the tendency to make evaluations is common in almost all interchanges of language, it is very much heightened in those situations where feelings and emotions are deeply involved ... So the stronger our feelings, the more likely it is that there will be no mutual element in communication .... This tendency to react to any emotional, meaningful statement and forming an evaluation of it from our own point of view is, I repeat, the major barrier to interpersonal communication.
>
> But is there any way of solving this problem, of avoiding this barrier? Real communication occurs and

this evaluative tendency is avoided when we listen with understanding. What does this mean? It means to see the expressed idea and attitude from the other person's point of view, to sense how it feels to him, to achieve his frame of reference in regard to the thing he is talking about.

Rogers, 1961

Yes, the distance between people isn't measured in feet but in minds. As skilled communicators to animals we know how to invite a wild fowl closer by using understanding or smooth movements. The motivating leader de-escalates the angry team, family, or business member by understanding. De-escalation involves turning words into feelings instead of proving wrong or calling guilty until proven innocent.

When facing complaints on possible escalation of conflicts remember these two paths:

Complaint

1. Judge—You're right or you're wrong based on my perspective.

1. Tries to understand—I'll look at your perspective.

2. Communicate understanding by turning words into feelings.

3. Ask for feedback "Do I understand correctly?"

4. Move toward conflict resolution by asking for same understanding that you gave.

De-escalating is a leadership approach to use when there is an emotional crisis to address. Understand the feelings of the other and temporarily throw away the gavel.

How could you use de-escalating as a leader in your organization?

5. Exposing

Exposing involves sharing the pressures and demands that the leader experiences with the other members of the organization. The goal of exposing is to help people see the situation from a newer, different perspective. Since the "law of myopia" suggests that people are more fully aware of the pressures that they themselves face than they are of the pressures faced by people on different levels than themselves, exposing is a natural eye-opener. Some of the myopia can be removed by exposing the members to new perspectives. Knowledge is almost always better than lack of it.

Despite the powerful effects that exposing can have, many leaders resist it out of fear. "What if they get to know as much as I know?" or "Will they recognize my flaws if they see more of the picture?" These are two reasons why leaders keep to themselves the facts that could be understood by all. The leaders fail to realize that in some cases, the more people know about the total picture the more empathetic and helpful they can become.

The owner of a skin care salon had employees who were disgruntled over their earnings. They argued that it was unfair that they, who did most of the work, made only fifty percent commission. The owner would just take the other fifty percent from the total service dollars. In fact, one of the skin care technicians was on the verge of quitting, hoping to open up another salon and get the full 100 percent. The owner didn't know where to turn since the accountant said that it would be impossible to raise any of the employees' commissions and continue to make a 9 percent profit. But on the other hand the owner didn't want to lose the personally trained employees—along with their clientele.

The frustrated owner attended a small business management seminar and voiced this dilemma. The consultant responded, "Have you shared with your people the bottom line facts of your business?"

"Of course not, that's really none of their business," the owner responded. "But, you see the more fully aware they are about the real facts, the more likely they will understand your situation. Without full awareness they will naturally tip the scales of justice in their favor. The more exposure they have to the total picture, the more likely a fair settlement through understanding can take place."

The open-minded owner decided to use the exposure approach to enlighten the employees and shared with them the original cost of thousands of dollars to open up the salon. The owner also pointed out that if this money had been put into Certificates of Deposit (10 percent), the earnings would have been more than the bottom line 9 percent profit. When the owner broke out the financial percentages of the business with its salary, insurance, rent, heat, telephone, skin care products, electricity, maintenance, and so on, the technicians' eyes were opened to a new way of looking at the total picture. Exposing made the difference.

As you may have noticed, Exposing is the inward reversal of the transferring approach. What a combination of ways to bring about mutual understanding by exposing the factors and your pressure points to the membership!

What are some ways you could use the approach of Exposing as a leader?

_____

_____

_____

6. Linking

Some researchers have argued that more people leave a particular job because of social factors than because of inability to handle the job. Clearly many people leave organizations because of feelings of not belonging to the group. And anyone who has ever been in a group where they felt they had little in common with the others knows the discomfort of feeling on stage alone.

Linking is the process whereby a leader identifies similarities amongst the membership to help everyone feel linked. Linking grew out of the social-psychological concept entitled "the similarity-liking effect." The "similarity-liking effect" suggests that the more familiar we are with something the more we tend to feel comfortable with it, and the more we perceive ourselves to be similar to another the more we like them.

A natural xenophobia—fear of the differences in other people—exists in many people in organizations. The newcomer, the isolate, are all human resources that are lost because they are "outsiders." Outsiders are in many cases afraid to make contributions because they are functioning at the safety level. Once their safety and social needs are met they move on to fulfill higher self-esteem and self-actualization needs (Maslow 1954). They can contribute without fear because they belong. The membership xenophobia is cured and outsiders become insiders. That process can be facilitated by linking.

Some forms of linking include:

1. Linking with past experience.

"Sal, you're from Des Moines, aren't you? Did you know (pointing) that Roger is from Decorah, Iowa?"

"Well, looks like we have two Drexel University graduates here. Did you folks know each other before?"

2. Linking with common interests.

"I know that Tom would agree with you, Sara, that the Dodgers will win the World Series—Tom often gets down to the stadium."

"Another movie-buff in our organization."

3. Linking with family similarities.

"You have twins also, Carol, don't you?"
"Ben and Joan just had twins last December."

56

"Did I hear you say you are going to the Marriage Encounter, Pete? Paul and Betty went last year and they had a great experience."

"Oh, yes, they say the 'terrible twos'. I think I know what you're going through with your little one, Jim."

4. Linking with common struggle.

"Our goal is to score this touchdown. We have two minutes. If we score we win. We need everyone's best effort in their unique positions. If everyone gives their total best for two minutes, we as a team, can turn this three point deficiency and march off victorious. That's our challenge."

"Diane, I know how it must hurt to have been turned down for that promotion. You certainly had a right to feel disappointed. The same thing happened to me a few years ago and I was devastated for about a month. Then I realized that that attitude was getting me nowhere but only making me more bitter. So I put it into second gear, came back and it was a result of that new attitude that I eventually did get this promotion. So I know that now it hurts a lot, but just as the leaves grow back on the trees in the spring, there is a tomorrow."

Linking unites the divided, it warms the cool, and it can erase some of the uncomfortable ambiguities that we feel toward those we really don't know. By pointing out similarities we humanize "the other," making them similar to us. We can then identify with at least a part of them—and they are part of us. We all become stronger when we are all part of the link provided by the leader.

How could you use a form of Linking amongst your people to bring about greater understanding and harmony?

_____

_____

_____

_____

1. Remember: Many leaders feel that too much of their time is spent on dealing with problems as a result of misunderstandings and poor communications, so, if this is true for you
Do: Make a decision today to be a communications troubleshooter in your department. Ask yourself, "Would a little effort today save me everyday problems in the long run?" And "Is it worth my time to improve understandings and communications with my people?"

2. Remember: In the healthy organization people tend to be in harmony, and there exists a desire for mutual trust. The harmonious organization does not happen haphazardly but is a result of a leader's plan, so
Do: Assess your organization to develop a sense of whether it is moving away from harmony or toward harmony.

    a. Do I really understand the pressures and frustrations on my people?

    b. Do they really understand the pressures and frustrations I face?

    c. Do my employees understand the pressures and frustrations that each other faces?

3. Remember: The main ingredient present in encouraging leaders is their ability and willingness to listen. Empathic listening involves understanding rather than immediately judging the world of the other, so
Do: Practice empathic listening today. When an employee speaks with you try to understand what he or she is saying from his or her perspective. Withhold judgment until the person has completed his or her position.

4. Remember: After you listen empathically and do an I to You Transfer with the discouraged person, you are in an extremely strong position to motivate because you understand them, so
Do: Identify the pressures, frustrations, needs and goals of your most discouraged person.

5. Remember: Relationships can be defined as being of either an I–it or an I–You nature. In I–it rela-

58

tionships, we tend to see other people as "its" or we give a diagnosis. On the contrary, in I–You relationships, we can Un-Diagnose and the other is viewed as a human with hopes, dreams, goals, pressures, and frustrations, so

Do: Experience your employees' worlds as if you were actually them. Do transfer with especially the discouraged person to understand him or her more effectively.

6. Remember: Misunderstandings are often the result of the myopia that exists amongst people in different jobs, so

Do: Make a plan to have people who are doing one job experience the world of people who are doing another job.

7. Remember: Often times peoples' actual surface behavior and emotions are only marks of their real selves.

Do: Instead of responding to the surface, peek beyond the surface and look for the underlying emotion, for example, anger may be, in fact, really hurt.

8. Remember: The more the members of your organization feel others are similar to them the more they will allow them inside their world, so

Do: Link your people by identifying similarities amongst them.

9. Remember: Just as a hitchhiker must put a thumb to the air to indicate a need, express your needs, frustrations, pressures and goals to your people, so

Do: Make sure that your people transfer to your world experience the pressures on you. You do this by exposing them to the pressures on you.

10. Remember: Your leadership style makes the difference on motivating unproductive people who are basically discouraged. Your encouragement is the antidote to discouragement, so

Do: Encourage by first of all understanding the real world of your people and seek the same in return. Create an encouraging atmosphere.

The Motivating Leader Is a People Builder

When you observe uplifting leaders, whether they be managers, parents, coaches, or even presidents, you consistently see a common ingredient present in their philosophy of people. Motivating leaders believe that you don't build people up by tearing them down. Uplifting people are human stimulants who believe that taller structures are built by construction instead of destruction. They, like effective parents, raise their people, not lower them. The reason true motivating leaders spend so much energy on people development is because they see that the success of their organization is related to the strengths and resources of its people. When people feel themselves encouraged to grow and encouraged to contribute, they function at higher levels using more of their resources in creation and less in defense. The motivating leader is a people builder who is always on the "construction" site. Unfortunately, in our questionnaires to people we found that most people had leaders and managers who tried to motivate out of threats, criticism, nitpicking, and flaw-finding or mistake-hunting. Why is it that so many leaders lose their positive potential to influence by taking the people destruction course?

Mistaken Leadership Beliefs on How To Motivate

Think of past leaders or managers that you've experienced who were so in tune to mistakes and aloof to the things you did correctly. Why did they somehow or another not sense the obvious, that motivation through intimidation, fear, or negativism was at best, temporarily successful. But tense leadership is destructive and leads to either poor morale or passive aggressiveness. There are a number of reasons they were unaware of better ways and it will serve us well to take just a few seconds to discover their mistaken thoughts before going into positive people building.

MISTAKEN LEADERSHIP BELIEF 1

If anything goes wrong, I, as the leader, will be blamed, so I must live over my peoples' shoulder and watch them every step of the way to quickly point out their mistakes. (Threatened)

MISTAKEN LEADERSHIP BELIEF 2

It is my job as leader to know more than anyone else. Since I am supposed to be the expert here, I can show my expertise best by criticizing, correcting, and spotting weakness. (Know-it-all)

MISTAKEN LEADERSHIP BELIEF 3

Spotting disabilities, inefficiencies, and flaws was the way I was raised, and look at me today. Besides, if you build peoples' egos up, they'll get swelled headed and become unmanageable. (Dominator)

MISTAKEN LEADERSHIP BELIEF 4

I assume a perfect performance. Why should I point out when they do what was expected of them? And anyway, a paycheck is all they need to be motivated. (Perfectionist)

The Threatened Leader

When a leader is under perceived threat, (whether the threat is real or not, doesn't matter) the stress experienced causes the person to react to errors in an exaggerated way. Any mistake is magnified. Instead of dealing with an error in a rational way (let's correct it, or at least make the best out of where we are right now) threatened leaders deal with the mistake irrationally (name calling, withdrawing, sulking, revenge).

Tension builds in an organization led by a threatened leader. Although I am aware of no research to support it, I would be curious to see if threatened leaders produce more turnover of personnel and more emotional problems in the ranks. Certainly threatened leaders of organizations where people volunteer and can quit at will lose their power because they lose their membership. This result has been observed in everyday life by many people.

What the threatened leader is unaware of is that the power to solve organizational problems exists within its people. People under threat live defensively. Defensive people can't create. The creation of new ideas is the answer to the mistakes. So threatened leaders find themselves in a Catch-22 situation. They receive no new ideas by membership who is threatened; no new ideas, no progress. As Tom Peters and Robert Waterman, authors of *In Search Of Excellence* have pointed out in a study of America's top corporations, good companies allow and even encourage mistakes, hoping that their decisions are right more than 50 percent of the time. Threatened leaders want 100 percent right decisions. So they make none at all. Threatened leaders truly do make less mistakes!

The Know-It-All Leader

Know-it-all leaders are threatened also and try to cover up their feelings of inadequacy by believing the impossible notion that "I must know more than anyone else here since I am the expert. If anyone challenges an idea of mine, it is a personal attack on me. If anyone asks me a question that I don't know the answer to, my leadership will be up for challenge. I can avoid being challenged by attacking first and spotting their weaknesses. I can spot something wrong that they did, and it will establish me as superior. The more I show them how wrong they are, the more they will respect me."

The newly appointed elementary school principal sought psychotherapy because of feeling threatened and caught into the know-it-all syndrome.

"You see Doctor, I had taught fifth grade, and while I did that for years and was good at it, now as principal, I don't know anything about kindergarten, first, second, third, fourth, and sixth grades. I live in constant fear that one of my teachers may come into my office and ask me a question about their grade and what they should be doing. And what if I don't know the answer? I just know that the teacher would go running to the faculty room and tell everyone that I, the principal, didn't even know."

"I think you have it wrong, Jim. Your job as principal is not to know more than the kindergarten teachers. If there is an expert in kindergarten in your school, that expert better be in the kindergarten classroom! Your job as leader is to help them become experts in what they do by building them, encouraging them to develop better ideas, and motivating them. A leader is an expert—an expert in motivating people. You are putting too much of a burden on yourself and making what could be an exciting and challenging job a painful experience."

The Dominating Leader

Some leaders believe it is their role to spend most of their energies correcting because of cultural reasons. It is the way much of society functions and so most of the models in the lives of dominating leaders were correctors. Parents tell the young child who puts her shoes on for the first time all by herself "they're on the wrong feet," rather than "wow, you put your own shoes on all by yourself, what an achievement for a three-year-old! Can you show us how you did that?"

School teachers tend to mark the number of wrong answers instead of the number of correct answers. Police give tickets for speeding as opposed to rewarding trophies or certificates for staying within legal limits. Public park signs read "no fires, no alcohol, no littering," rather than "enjoy yourself, experience the beauty of the green grass and the clear blue mountain lake." Weather forecasters tell us there is a 20 percent chance of rain, not 80 percent chance of sunshine, and people who give you directions tell you to turn at the fourth red light. Why do they pessimistically conclude that all of those lights will be red? There is a 50 percent chance they'll be green! All of these are examples of a cultural bias toward negative focusing.

The dominating leader hasn't taken time to break out of the cultural mold and responds like everyone else does. If one takes just a few minutes to think of it, there are alternative ways of leading people and of building them to strengthen the total organization. In a few pages some alternative ways of building people will be discussed, but first consider the fourth mistaken belief of discouraging leaders, perfectionism.

The Perfectionist Leader

The perfectionist leader assumes that everyone will do a perfect job and that they need no recognition for their efforts and for their achievements. "Only weaklings need a pat on the back," or "If you compliment someone, you are likely to spoil them," or even "a paycheck is the only reward a person needs," are some of the naive conclusions drawn by discouraging leaders. In *Turning People On*, I suggested that positive information that a leader has about a person's achievements is meaningless until it is communicated to that person. "Silence is not golden" when we want to encourage people. The encouraging leader does not assume that people know they are doing well. Failure to communicate positives may lead to discouragement. Consider the possibility that many people go through an entire day without any encouragement. Someone cooks meals, someone does his or her homework, someone takes out the garbage, and so on. These roles are frequently not acknowledged, just assumed.

In organizations, people start to withdraw their services or slack off when unmotivated. Confrontation may then be the only intervention that appears appropriate. It could have been avoided by a more positive style that didn't assume perfection but appreciated it and showed it.

Motivating leaders avoid leadership problems by building people. In this chapter we discuss eight approaches to being an uplifting leader who builds people.

These approaches may be appropriate for the following problems:

1. Morale problems
2. Lack of confidence
3. Burnout
4. Perfectionism
5. Negative self-image
6. Feeling of insignifiance, unimportance
7. Lack of motivation
8. Irresponsibility
9. Promoted people in new levels of responsibility

Eight approaches to people building
1. Re-imaging
2. Image Analyzing
3. Asset-focusing
4. Converting
5. Special-izing
6. Best Foot Forwarding
7. Un-assuming
8. Underwhelming

7. Re-imaging

The major cost of the "building up by tearing down" leadership approach is on the self-images of the membership. And it is this, the self-image that has been demonstrated to be the major determinant on achievement and performance.

The leader who believes in building people starts by building the self-image or re-images the unmotivated. Re-imaging grew out of the work of Maxwell Maltz, the plastic surgeon who wrote *Psychocybernetics*. Maltz concluded:

When self-image changes, everything in life changes. Researchers have shown that students have gone from "F" grades to "As" in a matter of weeks. Salespeople have literally doubled their income, shy people have become respected leaders, depressed people have developed a renewed enthusiasm for life. (Maltz 1960)

All of these changes took place because of changes in self-image or re-imaging. One study after another has demonstrated the power of one's self-image on performance. Self-image appears to be even more important than I.Q. in determining achievement. W. B. Brookover and his associates concluded from their studies that changes in a person's self-image lead to changes in achievement (Brookover, et al. 1962). Again, this is powerful news. A motivating leader, a builder of people, realizes that performance is preceded by the belief—"I can." K. L. Harding, another researcher, showed that it could be predicted with reasonable certainty whether a student would or would not quit school just by knowing the student's self-image. (Harding 1966)

A better gauge than any test devised of how a person will perform in a position is the person's self-image. On these astounding findings, the father of self-image research, William Purkey, in relation to achievement (school) and self-image writes:

The conclusion seems unavoidable—a student carries with him certain attitudes about himself and his abilities, which play the primary role in how he or she performs in school. (Purkey 1970)

Did you ever see a person labeled stupid or retarded by one person (leader) in the presence of another person who believed in him or her? This same person performed like two different people in the two different settings. He or she performed at a higher level in the presence of the believer. The believer was a builder of self-image. Maltz wrote:

> *The self-image is the key to the personality and to human behavior. Change the self-image and you change the personality and behavior. But more than this, the self-image sets the boundaries of individual accomplishment. It defines what you can and cannot be. Expand the self-image, and you expand the area of the possible. The development of an adequately realistic self-image will seem to imbue the individual with new capabilities, new talents, and literally turn failure into success.*
>
> Maltz 1960

Keep in mind the power of self-image on achievement that these research studies indicate. A negative-oriented leader literally alters self-image in negative directions causing anxiety, apprehension, and feelings of incompetence, all inconsistent with long-term performance. It can be otherwise—through a re-image approach of leadership.

SELF-IMAGE: A PERSON'S SELF-DEFINITION

Think of self-image this way: Imagine that a *Webster* dictionary representative came to you and said, "I'd like to put you in our dictionary next year, and like all words in our dictionary have a definition behind their names, we will need you to define yourself, so that the world can know you. For example,

> *pencil*—a rod-shaped object filled with graphite or lead, used to write with.
>
> *Nick Harris*—an intelligent person who at times lacks confidence. He also panics when he makes a mistake. He tends to be shy with people.

The self-definition is the self-image. It is not accurate, but the actor believes it is accurate, and then proceeds through life treating the self-image as a fact. The self-image grew from past experience.

Second grade teacher: "Nicholas, you are a bright lad."

Sales manager to Nick: "Nick, your biggest problem is that you lack confidence and will never get anywhere without confidence." (Manager's theory is "I can scare him into getting confidence," or the building up by tearing down syndrome.)

Mother and Father: "Nick, unless you do something perfectly, don't do it at all." (panics when making mistakes)

Girlfriend: "Nick, you are so shy with people. Why don't you come out of your shell?"

Nick's self-definition today, then, is a result of many social experiences. Remember an encourager's five Insights, and the importance of people on people? The good news is that the leader is in an excellent position to build new, more constructive self-definition into Nick's personality. This is called "re-imaging." The balance of the approaches in this chapter are various ways for a leader to re-image, to build new self-definition to produce improved performance, and, to say the least, a happier, more confident life.

8. Image-analyzing

To re-image, the leader needs to be aware of the member's current self-image. This is achieved through an *image-analysis*. An image-analysis is an attempt to construct an individual's dictionary definition of who he or she is, including the positive and negative characteristics. An image-analysis can be done in one of two ways:

1. The leader can infer by observation of behavior some of the components of a person's self-image, or
2. The leader can actually ask members to write their own dictionary definition of themselves.

IMAGE-ANALYSIS BY OBSERVATION

A leader of a small business selling beauty products to others, who in turn sells notices that Carol, a 45-year-old woman who was originally turned on, has produced no sales for a month. The leader thinks back and remembers a few of Carol's latest statements:

"Well, I'm going through this divorce now and I have to admit that often times I wonder if I'm still attractive, and will I ever be loved again."

On another occassion, Carol said, "I took a chance and called this old college buddy up and invited him over for dinner and he turned me down. I never called again."

With these two thoughts in mind, the sensitive leader realized that Carol needed to be built up. Through the image-analysis some of Carol's self-definition may be:

Carol J.—unappealing (yet selling beauty products), rejected, gives up after being turned down, lacking determination.

The image-analysis helped the leader realize that Carol needed to be built up through re-imaging (see the oncoming approaches in the pages ahead). Re-imaging is a much better approach than pressuring, lecturing, or pointing out weaknesses.

IMAGE-ANALYSIS THROUGH
MEMBERSHIP PARTICIPATION

The leader at a staff meeting can encourage the members to do their image-analysis.

The leader requests:

I'd like you to imagine that a representative from the Webster's dictionary people came to you and said, We at Webster's would like to put your name in the dictionary next year but like all of our words, we need a definition behind your name so that the world will know who you are. What definition would you put in back of your name to describe you? Think of traits, and characteristics, for example, outgoing, shy, and so on.

The leader then encourages the membership to think of when and at what age these definitions became part of the individual self-image. By pointing out that the person wasn't born this way but became this way, the leader demonstrates that it is possible to develop new traits and characteristics during life.

The leader asks them to add some new definitions on to their self-image and eliminate those that are counter-productive. The leader then asks them how a new life would look if they were this new way. The membership is encouraged to think of opportunities to act, based on the new self-image, to make it happen. People are then encouraged to report at the next meeting progress they have made as a result of re-imaging.

9. Asset-focusing

Some leaders are hindered by their inclination to see liabilities and mistakes. They see in the old adage the glass of water half empty, rather than half full. These leaders tend to choose, select, or focus on the negatives. Negative-focusing builds negative self-images. Negative self-image produces behavior consistent with self-image.

"But," the owner and manager of the real estate agency said, "I have this one agent who has nothing, nothing good. What do I do to motivate him?" Think of that person who has nothing good about him or her. Slowly go over this list and see if any asset comes closer to being appropriate. Then record it.

_____

_____

_____

Start to lift up and bring in this down-and-out person by being an asset-focuser.

Asset-focusing is based on the concept of Field Theory developed by Kurt Levin, who believed that we have infinite ways of responding to any situation. We select

above board
absorbing
abstract thinking
academic, scholarly
accepting
accessible
accommodating
accountable
achieving
action-oriented
adaptable, flexible
advanced, ahead-of-
time
adventurous
affable
affectionate
alive
alongside
ambitious
amenable
amusing
approachable
artful
artistic
assertive
assiduous, hard-
working
astute
at ease
attentive
authentic
authoritative
aware
balmy, smoothing,
calm
benevolent
benign
big-hearted
blissful
broad-minded
busy
candid
capable
carefree
casual
cautious
character
charitable
charming
chic, fashionable
civil, polite
clarifier
clean

clear
clever
commanding
competent
comprehensive
concise
concrete-thinker
confident
congenial
conscientious
contemporary
content
cooperative
cordial
courageous
courtly
creative
credible
critical
cultured
curious
daring
dazzling
decent
decisive
deep-thinking
deliberate
demanding
demonstrative
dependable
determined
devout
didactic
diligent
direct
domestic
dramatic
dreamer
dynamic
earnest
easy-going
economical
educated
effective
effervescent
eloquent
enduring
energetic
enlightening
enterprising
enthusiastic
ethical
even

exacting
exhaustive
expedient
explicit
expressive
fair
faithful
fearless
fervent
forceful
forgiving
forward
frank
frugal
fun-loving
futuristic
gallant
generous
genteel
genuine
get-along
giving
good-hearted
good-natured
graceful
gracious
grateful
gregarious
growing
guardian
guiding
guileless
gutsy
happy
hard-working
hardy
harmless
harmonious
healthy
heartening
helper
heroic
honest
honorable
hope-giving
hospitable
humanitarian
humorous
hygienic
idealistic
imaginative
impartial
improving

improvising
indefatigable
independent
indispensible
individualistic
industrious
informed
ingenious
innocent
inspiring
instructive
intellectual
integrity
intense
interesting
introspective
inventive
invaluable
invigorating
involved
judicious
kind
knowledgeable
laborious
lawful
leadership
learned
lenient
level
liberal
lively
likeable
loyal
magnanimous
matter-of-fact
meaning-giving
mediating
merciful
methodical
mild
mindful
moderate
modern
modest
moral
mobile
motivated
motivator
neat
neighborly
negotiable
neutral, impartial
noble

nourishing
objective
observant
open
organized
original
outstanding
participator
peaceful
perceptive
persevering
persistent
persuasive
philosophical
plausible
pleasant
playful
poised
polished
popular
positive
potent
powerful
praiseworthy
practical
precise
prepared
productive
proficient
profound
progressive
promising
prompt
proper
prosperous
protector
provider
punctual
purposeful
questioning
quick-witted
quizzical
radiant
rapt
rational
realistic
reassuring
reasonable
refined
reflective
rejuvenating
reliable
religious

remarkable
remindful
reserved
resolute
respectful
respectable
responsible
responsive
sagacious
scholastic
scrupulous
seasoned
sedate
self-confident
self-control
sensitive
sincere
smooth
social
soothing
sophisticated
sparkling
specific
spirited
spontaneous
sporty
spunky
stable
stalwart
stately
staunch
stimulating
straightforward
strong
studious
sturdy
stylish
succinct
systematic
tactful
task-oriented
teamworker
technical
tenderhearted
thoughtful
thorough
timeless
tolerant
trained
tranquil
trendsetter
trustworthy
truthful

up-to-date	vocal	wholehearted
venturesome	watchful	willful
veteran	well-adjusted	wise
vibrant	well-read	witty
visionary		

what to focus on. Asset-focusing involves being tuned in to observing "what is right with" or "what is a potential resource of another person." Asset-focusing is an approach to help re-image an individual into a more positive self-image. Asset-focusing is a leader's way of building by constructing.

How could you as a leader make use of asset-focusing in your organization?

_____

_____

_____

10. Converting

What if, after going over the previous list, a leader concludes, "I still haven't identified any positive traits in this person to start to build him or her." Is hope lost? No, not for the creative motivating leader who wants to build. Converting is the next step. Converting is the process of changing negative traits by seeing the positive, applicable components of those traits and sharing the observation.

Look at the following negative traits and ask yourself if there is a positive silver lining in any of them:

1. Stubbornness _____

2. Lazy _____

3. Foolishly daring _____

4. Trouble maker _____

5. Nosey _____

6. Gabby _____

7. Impulsive _____

8. Nitpicker _____

Is stubbornness a negative trait? Yes, in a way, but many people would want their heart surgeon to possess this same very negative trait of stubbornness while operating on them.

Is foolishly daring a negative trait? Yes, but all of the world's great entrepreneurs and great scientists dared to tread on unsafe ground. Thank God, people like Columbus and Jonas Salk were foolishly daring.

The motivating leader who wants to build people can see things in them that others can't. A prison counselor—the best I've ever seen at converting—observed:

> *Yes, it is my job to help these prisonors leave jail and go out and function in the world. It's a hard task because their self-images are so negative that they believe they have no skills to offer society. So I take their very crimes and convert them to assets that may have been previously misdirected.*
>
> *The safe-cracker, for example, has manual dexterity, determination, courage, goal-directedness, dreams, love of work, wishes for a better tomorrow, hope, in many cases strong knees, good ears, ability to plan ahead, and certainly patience. I help them to see that if they take these same traits and channel them in the right direction, very few companies wouldn't want them.*

Convert the very liabilities of a person into assets that are socially constructive and build, build, build.

Reflect for a few moments and convert some of your people's liabilities into assets.

_____

_____

_____

11. Special-izing

Special-izing is the process of identifying one person's uniquenesses and sharing them with the person. These uniquenesses are captured by observing the person's claim to fame.

Each one of your people has a bit of pride about something that he or she does well. This magical motivated feeling of "I'm good at so and so" may have to do with some talent on or off the job. It really doesn't matter whether the person's claim to fame is "I'm really an organized person at work" or "I won the company golf tournament over the past two years" or even "I'm a great grandma." What does matter is that you communicate your awareness to his or her claim to fame.

What are claims to fame? Claims to fame are proud moments in peoples' lives of achievements or even current talents or skills that they have. Claims to fame are also the sources of personal feelings of competence and uniqueness.

Children readily share their claims to fame with others. "I can run faster than anybody on my whole block," or "I'm really good at spelling. I won the spelling bee!" Adults, however, are less likely to share their sources of pride or talent with others, either because they are not even aware of their talents or because they feel that others just don't care. Be a caring, sensitive leader by listening and watching your people with extended antennae that are fine-tuned to their sources of pride.

Watch how the listening manager differs from the discouraging manager in response to the same comments of an employee

Employee: You know my report that was due on Friday? I'll have it finished by Monday, four days earlier, Mr. Manager.

Discouraging Manager: Ok, well, let me give you another report to work on then.

Encouraging Manager (who is tuned into claims to fame): You finished the report already, Tom! Great! That will give me more time to review it. You have a real respect for deadlines. I know I can always count on you.

Look again at Tom's comment and the way he expressed his achievement. Wear claims to fame sensitive ears and eyes. Can you see and hear pride in Tom's accomplishment? The discouraging manager ignored the extra effort, leaving Tom with the feeling that going the additional mile wasn't worth it. If Tom stays with this manager, he may wind up on our list of burned-out discouraged employees in a short period of time. The claims to fame recognizing manager, in seeing Tom's pride in beating a deadline, turned it into a claim to fame. You can bet that Tom, in the future, will continue to reach deadlines because it is part of his claim to fame and he was recognized by an encouraging manager. Tom, as a result of an encouraging manager, is happy. Mr. Manager is happy, and the company is happy. Make your employees, yourself, and your company happy by recognizing your employees' claims to fame.

Where Can You Use Special-izing with a Member?

Sense sources of strength by identifying the hidden resources in your employees. Be a talent scout! Spot not only the assets that are obvious, but imagine what hidden resources, what undiscovered potential also might exist in your people.

At times you may feel that one of your people is suffering from an energy crisis. Solve the energy crisis almost instantly by identifying the potential resources in the discouraged employee. What are resources? Resources are the hidden assets that aren't immediately obvious.

Identify resources in some of your people.

_____

_____

_____

12. Best Foot Forwarding

Best foot forwarding is an approach to building people that could be credited to psychologist B. F. Skinner and used with baseball players in a slump. Best foot forwarding is allowing people who are feeling at their worst to reexperience themselves at their best by reinforcing past successes.

Successful, encouraging leaders deal with people quite differently than leaders of the past. Remember the old-time baseball manager, for example? Traditionally, baseball managers would spend most of their time explaining to the hitter who was in a batting slump what he was doing wrong. "You're stepping in the bucket. You're taking your eye off the ball. Don't drop your shoulder. Don't stand away from the plate. Are you afraid of the fastball?"

Step into the slumping hitter's spikes for a few moments and give yourself the experience of listening to your fault-finding manager's observations. Imagine that you have to step up to the plate against the league's toughest and fastest pitcher immediately after hearing these five comments from your manager. Do you feel that being bombarded by your manager's negative comments would make you more capable, more confident as you step into the batter's box?

> Maybe what the manager says is true. Maybe I am afraid of the fastball, but what if the ball is coming directly at me? What will I do? If I duck, the manager will be convinced that I'm gun shy and pull me out of the lineup. And if I don't duck, maybe I'll get beaned.

Not only does focusing in on what a person does wrong add confusion, anxiety, and tension, but most importantly it decreases the batter's self-confidence when stepping to the plate.

"I'm in a bad hitting slump. And I'll bet that I'll never break out of it with all of these things wrong with me."

Modern, encouraging baseball managers employ a more effective style to help a troubled batter out of a slump. Positive managers have video-cassettes of recordings of some of the hitter's finest moments. Prior to stepping up to the plate, the batter turns on the video-cassettes and watches his big hit, his winning grand slam or his perfectly placed bunt that brought the crowd on its feet and caught the dazzled opponent off his feet. The hitter hears his name announced over the public address system and steps up to the plate, this time, with confidence. And by observing what he did when his hitting was hot, the hitter subconsciously learns how to lift the shoulder, learns how to stand near the plate, and remembers to go after the fastball aggressively with the winning feeling. Be a modern, encouraging manager by pointing out the talents and assets of your people.

Start by seeing the one thing that Joe does right rather than the nine things that Joe does wrong. Then sit back and watch the strength and confidence you gave Joe propel him to try to improve number two, then number three, and so on. Give people the "I can do it feeling because there are a lot of things that are right with me. Let me put my best foot forward."

When can you use best foot forwarding with your membership?

_____

_____

_____

13. Un-assuming

Un-assuming relates to one of the five insights about people from Ch. 2—People are motivated by recognition. Un-assuming is the process of occasionally recognizing and not taking for granted the routine everyday actions of the membership.

Louise and Tom will never forget their un-assuming leader:

> *Louise, you have especially great talents in working with difficult clients. Your sensitivity in handling*

people is a real asset to us all. It's almost as if we have a resident psychologist here.

Anna, I never saw anybody who could find those lost policies like you can. I'd personally appreciate it if you would share some of the techniques you use with some of the other employees to help them.

Tom, thanks for keeping all of the spirits of the other real estate agents up during this difficult market time. Whenever you come into the office you give us drowning folks a periscope to rise above the water and see the land of hope.

The leaders of these three people could have held the comments in but instead chose to share the observations with Louise, Anna, and Tom. The leader was "in touch" with his or her positive influencing powers. Be a "pick em up type" type of person to your people. Don't assume—notice!

How could you make use of un-assuming?

_____

_____

_____

14. Underwhelming

Underwhelming is a people building approach I learned from a former dean with whom I worked. Gust Zogas didn't plan underwhelming to be a technique—it was a very natural style for him.

Underwhelming involves working with people with the opposite approach of bowling them over with your knowledge. Instead, underwhelming is turning to the membership for their knowledge. The underwhelming leader believes that the people in the organization have the capacity to come forth to answer the demands of a situation. Underwhelming is an approach that is limited to secure leaders. The underwhelming leader is strong enough to show weakness, secure enough to be real, and intelligent enough to know what he or she doesn't know.

Underwhelming builds people because the leader shows respect for them to play a part in finding a solution.

List some instances where you can employ underwhelming.

_____

_____

_____

Ten crucial things to remember
Ten practical things to do from Chapter 4
MOTTO: "Motivating leaders are people builders"

1. Remember: A survey conducted by People Media Inc. of Reading Pennsylvania revealed that almost every single respondent (employees) answered "Yes" to the question, "In your past, were you more motivated by leaders who saw your assets than your liabilities." So
Do: Put your eye on the positive to build.

2. Remember: Don't put extra undue pressure on yourself by believing, "I must know more than every person here," so
Do: Be prepared to learn from your people's ideas whenever possible. If you are asked a question to which you don't know the answer, simply respond, "I don't know. I will find out." What a non-defensive way of gaining respect!

3. Remember: The unmotivated person has a self-image problem which needs to be altered, so
Do: Begin a re-imaging program with your unmotivated or discouraged people to build them.

4. Remember: To re-image, you, the leader, must have some ideas about a person's current self-image, so
Do: Construct a self-image analysis or have the person construct his or her own self-image or dictionary definition. Add and remove. Make a self-improvement plan.

5. Remember: People's behaviors are functions of their self-images. Negative behavior is a product of a negative self-image, so
Do: Do an asset analysis by observing all of the assets in

this chapter that could be relevant to the individual and share them.

6. Remember: Even liabilities in people can be converted into assets to build them, so
Do: Take a person's very weakness and turn it into an asset by creative leadership. Show how that asset can tie into contributing to the organization's goals.

7. Remember: People have a need for uniqueness, so
Do: Specialize them by identifying their unique claims to fame or proud moments in their lives.

8. Remember: People who are down and out (slumping) will remain on the downhill unless someone turns them around, so
Do: Recall with them some of their finer moments and identify some of the assets these moments demonstrated they have. Put their best foot forward.

9. Remember: Humans have a strong need for recognition that is often lost in the routine, so
Do: Don't take performances for granted. Be an unassuming leader who recognizes and notices others' efforts.

10. Remember: Overwhelming people with your knowledge intimidates the membership, so
Do: Turn people on by underwhelming them, and allow them to help find the solution. What a way to build.

Motivating leaders build people.

Plant Positive Purpose
in People

A day that will stand out in the history books for centuries ahead is July 20, 1969. Recall what happened? It was a day when humankind's grasp became closer to its reach. It was a day when the citizens of the planet Earth placed their first person on the moon one quarter of a million miles away. A proud day for all earthlings.

July 20, 1969 was especially a proud day for me. Why should it have been more important for me than most others? All because of a special meaning-giving leader for whom I worked. Let me explain the power of a meaning-giving leader.

In the summer months of 1963-1967 I was employed by a Reading, Pennsylvania-based steel company, Carpenter Technology. My job responsibility was to bundle bars of steel over and over again for eight hours a day, five to six days a week. Sound boring? Could be, but I was fortunate enough to have a far-sighted foreman who helped point out to each of us bundlers what we were really doing.

"Part of what you guys will be bundling today is headed for Detroit and will be used for making automobiles," the burly enthusiast would say at the beginning of the day. On another occasion the seven-to-three crew was told that the steel bars we were bundling today were destined for a pharmaceutical company where they would be made into surgical equipment.

But the one meaning-giving day I remember the most was when Mr. U. confided, "This week most of what you fellas will be wrapping up to ship out is a specialty steel designed to be part of the spacecrafts like the one that our government will eventually be landing on the moon!"

Well, I hope it doesn't sound corny to say but on that July day when Neil Armstrong took his first step on the lunar surface, I was in the front row of the world's cheering section looking back with pride on my exciting moments of bundling steel bars from seven-to-three o'clock, five days a week. I often wonder how many tens of thousands of people like myself also made a contribution in some way, shape, or form—from secretaries to mail persons, to janitors, to the moon landing. Most of them, I'll bet, never experienced the pride I did. Why? Because most contributors didn't have a manager like Mr. U. who took the time to share with the employees how their jobs affect the people of the community—or humanity! The leader planted positive purpose in our work.

People Need Purpose and Meaning

Besides landing a man on the moon, the 1960s brought about some major changes in other areas of life. People began looking at life quite differently. This change was recognized in the offices of psychologists and psychiatrists in terms of their patients' symptoms. Carl Rogers, Abraham Maslow, Rollo May, Victor Frankl and many other observers of human behavior began writing about the problems expressed by the "new patients" in the 1960s. Instead of the traditional manic depressives or hysterical neuroses symptoms the new patient described another problem. This new phenomena was called by different names. Some called it "loss of meaning in life," "lack of purpose," "existential neuroses," "problems in living," "lack of will," "alienation," or "feelings of insignificance."

This disease was observed by some to be a function of a change in the thinking of people in society. The child-like existence whereby one gives up his or her will to society's authorities (the corporation, the government, etc.) characterized the 1950s. William H. Whyte described in *The Organization Man* the grey flannel suit decorated salesman whose every area of life was dictated by the corporation. Questions like "How should I dress?" Where should I live?" and "With whom should I socialize?" were all answered by the higher authorities. David Reisman in *The Lonely Crowd* describes the powerful push to conform, to act a certain way and to give up one's own creative ideas. The wife surrenders her life to a role around her children. Her children grow up and she becomes filled with an inner emptiness, wondering how to define herself now—since her only previous definition was mother. "What is my reason for being?" The home and the nest that the husband and wife worked so hard for years to build, giving them purpose then, now stood only as an empty remnant of past purposes. Indeed the song "Is that all there is?" was a ripe reflection of the feeling that when you put all of your purpose in life in one basket composed of a materialism, the material fades. Even gold medals fade. And even watches given at retirement stand only as poorly-timed reminders of a life governed by time clocks.

The former mother, strong enough to express her weaknesses and needs, goes back to school, begins reading, and seeing the psychologists to look for something more. She begins asking questions about who this person was that she saw when she looked into the bathroom mirror? Her teenager's toothbrushes gone and her sagging lines stand as a reminder that even beauty fades. She becomes aware that any value of life based on the material or the temporary loses its power by the day. What really counts is the purpose, the will, the meaning to be a part of, to contribute, to be, to understand. These are values of the metaphysical type—the long-lasting solid things one cannot see. If you are the leader of a volunteer organization, you can see her there in the second row buttoning the little boy's coat and asking him if he brushed his teeth that morning. If you are the manager of a restaurant you'll see her coaxing someone to have a second helping or today she, indeed, may be your own leader.

John Naisbitt, in his bestseller *Megatrends,* refers to our time as a time living in the parenthesis between the past and the future. Yes, of course there are uncertainties in the transition but the proud whitecaps of a whole new wave of meaning can be seen in the distance by the far-sighted. These difficult changes that people had to go through were indeed healthy ones in the long run. The changes—the demand for personal meaning in the home, the school, the church, the workplace, and the community were all positive symptoms that we were advancing to a new level of development. Our great-grandparents worried about their next meal. Life was, at best, a chore to make it through. Today people demand not just a "normal," life, not just to get by, but to seek fulfillment, meaning, purpose and significance. As a society we have moved towards what could be called "societal-actualization." Marilyn Ferguson in *The Aguarian Conspiracy* proclaimed that all of the para-digms, models, or rules for life are changing and the change is a good one—for everyone.

The leadership styles of the past based on autocracy, rigid roles, inflexibility and materialism will not work with this new person in the workplace who sees many optional approaches to a life of TV every night. This book's thesis concerning the style of a motivating leader is that to bring meaning and purpose to people in your organization is not just a good idea, or an afterthought, but lies at the very cornerstone of motivating people on the threshold of the twenty-first century. Maybe the word *cornerstone* in the previous sentence can be replaced with the word *heart.*

Leadership Means Giving Meaning and Purpose to People

In Search of Excellence, a book every leader might want to come close to memorizing, went to the bottom line question: What type of leadership works and what type doesn't work?

Poorer performing companies focus on the numbers rather than on the product and the people who make and sell it. The top companies, on the other hand, always seem to recognize what the companies that only set financial targets don't know or don't deem important. The excellent companies seek to understand that every man seeks meaning (not just the top fifty who are in the bonus pool).

Peters and Waterman, the authors, go on:

Nietzsche believed that "he who has a why to live for can bear almost any how." John Gardner observes in *Morale*, "Man is a stubborn seeker of meaning." (Peters & Waterman, 1982, p.76)

In *New Pathways in Psychology* author Colin Wilson wrote

> *Man evolves through a sense of external meaning. When his sense of meaning is strong he maintains a high level of will-drive and of general health. Without this sense of external meaning, he becomes a victim of subjective emotions, a kind of dream that tends to degenerate into nightmares.*
>
> Wilson, 1972, p. 39

And indeed I add, "If we don't have a purpose 'raising' us we are orphans to life."

Planting Positive Purpose in People

In this chapter some approaches to raise people will be suggested for you, the motivating leader, to help them answer the question, "Why do I toil?" This chapter is especially relevant for the following problems:

1. Burnout
2. Apathy
3. Closed-mindedness
4. Drug/alcohol problems
5. Organization stagnation
6. Loss of meaning

7. Questioning, "Why do I do this?"

8. Lack of motivation

Five meaning giving approaches

1. Home-ing in

2. Meta-job describing

3. Winding up

4. Before and aftering people

5. Un-menializing

15. Home-ing In

Home-ing in is a leadership tool designed to more effectively understand people by understanding their pressures, frustrations, and values outside of work. I learned about home-ing in as a guidance counselor when I wondered why some students performed nowhere near their potential. I decided to visit them in their homes. In the setting where they lived I listened to them reflect about the school. The insight shook me like the explosion of Mt. St. Helen's. Their lives outside of school were much more important in their life priorities. I would never have had that insight without home-ing in. I understood their situation and their lack of motivation more clearly. Lack of motivation is lack of meaning.

Think for a moment about some of your people. When they meet someone for the first time at a social gathering and are asked what they do for a living or what organization or hobbies they are involved in, do they put their fingers in front of their mouths and apologetically ramble a few words, quickly hoping that the conversation spotlight moves on to a more interesting, less ho-hum topic? Or, do their shoulders open up like a peacock displaying its feathered finery as they proudly speak of their contribution to the company, the team and society?

Through home-ing in, a leader can get an inside scoop from the outside. This gives the leader a better perspective to understand the feelings and meaning of the person, to find if he or she is fulfilled.

Use home-ing in with your most discouraged people. How do they describe their contribution to your organization to a friend?

_____

_____

_____

_____

16. Meta-Job Describing

The highly respected Springfield, Illinois barber-stylist was asked for the formula to his secret of success in giving haircuts. "Oh, I don't give haircuts," he responded, "I give courage and confidence and hope." He loved his work and he knew his contribution. That's why he was successful! He knew that the haircut was the physical thing that he did and he knew that a good haircut led to some results that went beyond the physical into the metaphysical.

The sensitive chief-of-police turned to his men and women after a tough holiday season when demands are placed heavily on them, and shared this thought: "Most of the community drove the roads and went to bed feeling safe this holiday season because of your efforts. A lot of people see you negatively, thinking that your job is to hassle and give tickets. But what you really give to most people is a feeling of security, justice, and caring—if they are wronged they call on you and you'll respond. The holiday season was better because of you. Thanks." Does a hairdresser give a haircut—or confidence? Does a law enforcement officer give tickets—or security? Does a teacher give discipline—or knowledge? Does the Statue of Liberty give a picture to take—or a theme of freedom to feel? Does a doctor give a checkup and a prescription—or a feeling of potential wellness? Do the Scouts give medals—or a feeling of competence? Does an artist give a painting or—inspiration? Does a coach give a strategy—or a winning attitude? Does a husband or wife give a paycheck at home—or love? Does a company give a paycheck alone or meaning with the paycheck? The difference between the physical and the metaphysical is above and beyond.

Give your people a raise, by showing how their efforts affect themselves, the organization and people in general. While employed as a consultant to a publishing company which had employees with low morale in the stock and order-filling departments, something struck me as quite interesting. In exploring their jobs with the resistant employees I discovered that the people didn't really know what a contribution they were making through their jobs.

In meeting with the workers I decided to "life-up" their jobs by helping them to see some of the "fringe benefits" of what they do. "Every day of your lives here at work is significant. Each and every day when you folks take books out of stock and send them out to successfully complete an order, some human being becomes satisfied. And each day there are people who await the arrival of their ordered packages of books. They need you! And each book that you send out has the capabilities of changing lives from depressions into joy, from boredom into meaning." I congratulated the people who are world changers and told them that each day they change the quality of people's lives. I concluded by adding that the people in their capacity have changed the quality of my life since I was an author—and the authors need them more than anyone! No stock people, no sales.

Because the stock and order-filling people were never told what a significant contribution their jobs made, their work and their feelings of satisfaction were reduced to simply putting books into boxes. Give your employees a raise by showing them how their efforts affect themselves, their organization, and humanity in general.

Meta-job Describing means seeing peoples' contributions at a higher level to instill purpose and meaning.

Responsibility	Physical	Meta-physical
switchboard operator	answer phones	first voice of the company
vitamin sales consultant	sells vitamins	_____

Responsibility	Physical	Meta-physical
secretary	types, files	_____
teacher	gives facts	_____
clergy	gives sermons	_____

How can you make use of Meta-Job Describing in your leadership capacity?

_____

_____

_____

17. Winding Up

When a clock stops ticking people think nothing about winding it up again. Burned-out people have stopped ticking. They need to be wound up. Winding up grew out of my curiosity of why people can't wait to see the next days' litanies of soap operas. Imagine if a leader could find the motivation behind people who cancel doctor appointments, tell noisy relatives to leave the house, and miss college classes to watch the soaps. That leader could create quite a motivated membership by understanding the principles soap operas use.

One of the techniques the soaps use is to get you excited about what will happen the next day. They wind you up. "Do you think Erik will say yes tomorrow?" or "John's wedding will be on tomorrow—I won't miss that to see if his ex-wife shows up." And then tomorrow they do the same to the viewer and God bless you on Friday because you have to wait three days instead of one to find out.

Soap opera writers are motivators. They give you a reason, a purpose, and a motive to tune in at any cost. They get you involved and build up anticipation. Winding up is the process of getting people to look forward to the day, a particular event, or giving them a reason, purpose, or motive to be present and to be involved. The leader shows them that there is something in it for them.

Effective leaders and great teachers—teachers who

take some time to tell their students about the special class the next day—are using Winding up. Imagine parents getting their little six-year-old wound up to go to school on a typical day by telling him something like this:

Jimmy, your dad and I are so excited for you because again today is another day of opportunity for you to get smarter—today is another school day. Imagine, honey, today you will learn new spelling words for a half an hour. You will be able to spell more words by this afternoon than you ever could in your whole life. And on top of that you will learn more about numbers for forty-five minutes. When you come home your dad and I would love to see our son count higher than ever before. And then to top it off you'll learn new things about the world of science. Remember that one day when you showed us how airplanes flew. Aren't you going to learn about the planets today? Maybe the teacher will talk about Star Wars! Yes, Jimmy, your dad and I are so proud of you. It's just too bad that some of these other first graders who are sick today won't learn all of those things. Well, son, we'll be waiting when you come home with some cookies and milk to sit down and listen to what you've learned today. Let us take one last look at you, because we will never see you the same again ... you'll be smarter!

Winding up is the style of inspiring leadership to help people find a reason, a purpose, or a motive to become involved. Winding up helps them see that "there's something in this for me" (other than just a paycheck or a fulfillment of an obligation).

How could you use winding up with your people?

_____

_____

18. Before and Aftering People

What do you know today that you didn't know yesterday? Last year at this time? Five years ago? When you were five? When you were born? You've come a long way, haven't you?

What will you know tomorrow that you don't know today? Next year at this time? Five years into the future? Ten years into the future? What could you know in your lifetime that you don't know now?

Before and aftering people is a concept that grew out of weight loss commercials, whereby people point out how they looked before and how they now look. The effectiveness of the before-after leadership approach is that it builds pride in self-development and growth, pride that is often neglected. Before and aftering people is the process of showing to the individual or the full membership where they were at some point in the past and where they have grown to be today.

Jill is a bit discouraged after a hard day. Her leader notices this and decides to before and after Jill the next day. The next morning her leader casually comments, "I have been thinking about you yesterday Jill and how far you've come since you've been here. I mean from trainee to student teacher, to crew chief to swing manager, assistant manager, and now manager! Incredible progress. At this rate where will you be in a year or two?" The vice-president of administration tells his general manager and managers, "Our department is the backbone and the supporting system of this company. My three year goal is for us to receive the respect we deserve and not take a back seat to any other department."

The vice-president is using, in this case, the *before* as today and the *after* as in the future. In this form, before and after-ing people has the effect of motivating to achieve future goals. They now have a purpose. How can you use Before and After-ing in you organization?

---

19. Un-menializing

In 1983 an aircraft dropped over a Southern U.S. state killing many people. The problem was traced to an overlooked seemingly trivial part of an airplane. Sometimes little things mean a lot.

The heart surgeon conducted 10 bypass operations a week for five years, a total of 2000 plus. The complicated task had become routine, and believe it or not, he was starting to become bored.

All jobs if done over and over gain can lead one to put him or herself on automatic pilot and forget an oil seal on an airplane or overlook a possible heart complication during surgery.

Leaders un-menialize when they occasionally remind the memberships of the importance of their contribution to the organization, the overall society, and their own development. General rule of thumb is that the more routine a responsibility is, the more the leader needs to un-menialize the task. It is especially important when quality appears to be slipping. In these instances the leader shows the membership the *positive implications* of good quality on the organization, the community, and on them.

Think of all of the different titles of people who look to you for leadership. How could you un-menialize the burned-out?

Title	Un-menializing plan
_____	_____
_____	_____
_____	_____

Ten crucial things to remember
Ten practical things to do from chapter 5

1. Remember: Society is changing drastically and while people were formerly motivated by just material gains, today people want meaning and purpose in their lives, so
Do: Be the leader who plants positive purpose.

2. Remember: Alienation and burn-out are the results of lack of personal meaning in what one does, so
Do: Let pictures of each of your people flash through your mind as though they were on slide carousels. Be an outsider, go to their home and ask each one the question, "How important is your work?" (home-ing). Imagine each

person's response. This will be a starting clue to you in whose spirits meaninglessness is living. Jot the names down of those who need a "booster shot" from you.

3. Remember: Lift discouraging spirits by giving them meaning and purpose in what they do. First of all, have genuine meaning and purpose yourself, so

Do: Make sure you believe in the importance of your own responsibilities. If you feel ho-hum about the significance of what you do the contagion of the yawn will be witnessed throughout the people environment.

Second, walk with the conviction that what we do is important.

Third, talk up the importance and significance of specific projects, for example, "This year our company is turning its eyes to you people to find new ways of . . . ."

Fourth, when you lose meaning and purpose have a built-in plan to fire up your spirits again, for example, further education, motivation classes, and so on.

4. Remember: The motivated person is one who feels "what I do is important," so

Do: Dig deeper into what each of your employees "actually" does (Meta-job Describing). Do this by thinking about the importance of what each person contributes.

5. Remember: There are many ways of looking at any job. The drab leader inspires in black and white, the meaning-giving leader inspires in rich shades of color, so

Do: Develop a job in its fullness:

Drab manager sees job	*Meaning giving manager sees meta-job describing*
1. a switchboard operator	1. the first voice of the company
2. a secretary	2. the very vehicle of communication to the outside world
3. a teacher	3. a molder of the future
4. a salesperson	4. the key to the company's future

See a responsibility in its colorful fullness and communicate your meaning to each specific position. Jot down every level you now have and write the specific job, not in just a simple black and white description but put your meaning-giving ad in "color."

6. Remember: In the old days, when a car broke down, an ineffective way to get it working again was to blame it and kick it. The effective way to get it started was to grab the crank and wind it up, so
Do: Wind up your burned out people. Enthuse them about what they will learn and achieve. Give them meaning, purpose, and a motive to be there.

7. Remember: One way of building trust and also to plant positive meaning and purpose in people is to be a credit-giving leader, so
Do: Never miss a single opportunity to give public and private credit to the achievers, idea-givers, and every contribution from the stamp licker to the janitor.

8. Remember: Sometimes people can't see themselves progressing and find themselves in a rut, so
Do: Before and after them by enthusiastically pointing out their progress (in position, in skills, in attitude) since they joined the organization.

9. Remember: People make the difference in the achievement of the organizational goals, so
Do: Show your employees how they have "made the difference" by pointing out to them very specific instances where their efforts brought about the achievement of goals (Un-menialize).

10. Remember: Often times your people will not understand why you ask them to do something that appears to be "just additional grief" or the "hard way." The reason for this lack of understanding is that they don't have your perspective. When this lack of understanding occurs, people become discouraged and feel that you are just giving them extra hassles, so
Do: Un-menialize by giving your people purpose to go the extra mile by showing them, very specifically, why you have to take the long road this time. Help them to see that

you, too, would like shortcuts but sometimes this extra effort is necessary.

Plant positive purpose in people. Spark your people's positive attitudes by bringing meaning into the organization. Now, keep the fires within your people stoked by communicating your belief in them and your positive expectations of their achievements.

Create a Winning Feeling

Goethe the poet suggested, "If you want someone to develop a specific trait treat them as though they already had it." In *In Search of Excellence*, Peters and Waterman state, "Label a man a loser and he'll start acting like one." In their study of the characteristics and attitudes present in America's top corporations, Peters and Waterman concluded:

> *The message that comes through so poignantly ... is that we (employees) like to think of ourselves as winners. The lesson that the excellent companies have to teach is that there is no reason why we can't design systems that continually reinforce this notion: most of their people are made to feel that they are winners.*
>
> Peters & Waterman, 1982

That winning mood is best determined by leadership's attitude and expectations. Low expectations communicate a disbelief in people. Respect, contrarily, is a belief communicated by leadership that "I believe in you, you people are made of the stuff that gets things done." The winning coaches always expect to win—they show it, they act it, they communicate it. In the back of your mind your probably suspected Namath and the Jets were going to win that Super Bowl. In watching the Nixon–Kennedy

97

debate you knew that Kennedy was a winning leader who could create a winning feeling in people. Winning leaders expect the best from their people—and more often than not, get the best.

Losing leaders don't expect to win. They tolerate minimum performance, ignore small successes to build bigger successes. They aren't present on the scene to inspire, to urge onward. Leaders who create the losing feeling are satisfied with the status quo. Isn't it amazing how we have come to accept mediocrity and accept less than 100 percent performance?

Phil Crosby, author of *Quality Is Free*, describes how in most instances we expect mistakes and aren't even disappointed when they happen. We get a bicycle with a few parts missing. Our meal is served cold, the carpet arrives in the wrong color, the salesman makes twelve instead of fifteen calls, the doctor arrives twenty minutes late, the switchboard operator cuts us off, the service station attendant gets gas on our car, our order is misunderstood, the secretary in the emergency room doesn't smile. Crosby goes on to say that quality of service and performance is not something out of the ordinary—it's not an extra, it's not just a good idea—it is simply giving people what they expect, what they paid for or what we in our contract agreed to—no more, no less.

A MacDonald's, Burger King, or Wendy's hamburger is quality because it is consistent and varies little each time. It's what we expect. Leadership demanded that standard of quality and went about making it happen. That is why very few of these major chains close down—leadership set a goal, expected the goal to be achieved and believed in its people. There are many examples of successful leaderships.

Disney didn't want Disneyland or Disneyworld to become a dirty amusement park. Compare the cleanliness there to the cleanliness of any major city.

Fred Heineken didn't want one bad bottle of beer—ever. How many bad bottles of Heineken have you ever experienced?

Willard Marriott Sr., now in his mid–80s, panics at the thought of one of his lobbies being dirty. Up until a few years ago he read every single customer complaint card in his two billion dollar-a-year operation. (Peters & Waterman, 1982)

Leadership's communicated expectations are the major factor in determining the performance and the winning or losing attitude of the membership. The influence of one's expectation on others is demonstrated not just in the corporation but in education, psychotherapy, and medicine as well.

Expectation and Teacher Leadership

Research studies have shown that teachers who have positive expectations from students actually produce greater student achievement, (Rosenthal & Jacobsen, 1968). When phoney psychological reports were given to teachers telling them that an individual's I.Q. was higher than it really was, the teachers' elevated expectations of the student's ability led to greater student achievement. In *The Unconscious Conspiracy: Why Leaders Can't Lead,* Warren Bennis states: In a study of school teachers, it turned out that when they had high expectations of their students, that alone was enough to cause an increase of twenty-five points in the students' I.Q. scores.

Robert Schuller, founder of the concept of "possibility thinking," reported on an elderly school teacher from New York who had such a high rate of success with students whose peers had a much higher frequency in brushes with the law. What was her success a result of? She said, "I just loved those kids and believed in them."

If someone believes in me and communicates that belief in my assets to me along with understanding, and a feeling that what I do is important, I will have a tendency to take a second look at myself. Down deep I want them to be right, so I may try to make it happen. And the fact that some psychologists tell us that we use only five to ten percent of our potential demonstrates that there always stands room for improvement—in the context of an encouraging leader or teacher.

Expectation and
Pyschotherapeutic Leadership

What the teacher expects is more often than not, what they will get. But the power of expectation goes way beyond the classroom and extends into the counseling therapist's office. Frieda Fromm-Reichman concluded that the major factor in determining whether a patient would or would not get better is the psychotherapist's expectations about the patient's prognosis. (Fromm-Reichman, 1950) The leader in the therapist's office can literally communicate a winning or losing feeling with the patient almost unobtrusively. "You're the kind of person who can pull yourself out of depression. You can get yourself out of the house, join a social organization, get out to meet people, develop your writing skills that you gave up in this depression. I believe in you." Or, "You're now too fragile to go out on your own."

This power of people on people is totally consistent with the social-comparison theory as advanced by Leon Festing. Basically, Social Comparison Theory argues that humans, in the absence of some objective standard by which they can evaluate themselves, will compare themselves to other fellow humans. It is from this comparison that they draw their conclusion about their worth. (1954) When the psychotherapist, an objective standard, communicates a respect for the patient, that person is more likely to move toward fulfilling those expectations. A therapist can communicate a winning feeling. What the therapist expects is, more often than not, what he or she will get.

Expectation and Medical Leadership

In *Persuasion and Healing* (1960), Jerome Frank discusses the power of the doctor's expectations on the patient's cure. Numerous studies describe the effects of the placebo—a sugar pill—along with guarantees from the doctor that "this will eliminate your symptoms." The

MD's communication of these expectations plays a role in the cure.

In fact, the popular writer Norman Cousins in his book *Anatomy of an Illness* described how he was told he had a disease that had never been cured before. How's that for creating hopeless expectation and a losing feeling? Well, Norman Cousins was fortunate enough to find a doctor with positive expectations and feelings of hope. These positive expectations became the sources of energy that propelled Cousins onward to search for the answer. He concluded that if negative thinking and a negative environment could produce symptoms of disease, could the reverse be true? Could surrounding oneself with the positive environment lead to good health? He started his "laughing cure" by bringing in Allen Funt of Candid Camera. Cousins took massive dosages of Vitamin C. He checked out of the hospital. Today Norman Cousins is totally cured of a disease that no one else ever lived through. He tried new approaches because he had a medical leader who gave him hope and the winning feeling. And as John Dryden wrote: "When there is no hope there can be no endeavor." I'd like to add: When there is some hope there may be an endeavor. I always liked "maybes" better than "no's."

Leaders create moods through their communicated expectations. Tolerance of less than the best is a clear message. Inspiring by striving for excellence, building pride, communicating respect, and showing confidence creates the winning feeling.

Creating a Winning Feeling by Expecting the Best

The fields of education, psychotherapy and medicine have demonstrated the importance of creating a winning feeling by expecting the best. To those fields we could add athletics, parenting, friendship, and any other area where two people meet and communicate expectations and ideas about the other.

Great leaders have great expectations. This chapter

lists a number of approaches to create a winning feeling with the membership by expecting the best. This chapter is particularly relevant for the following people challenger:

1. Low self-esteem
2. Loss of belief in a particular person
3. Irresponsibility
4. Poor work quality
5. Low morale
6. Excuses
7. Feelings of being overwhelmed by problems
8. The "low on the totem pole" feeling

Four approaches to create a winning feeling

1. Respect-ability
2. Delegating
3. "Can" Opening
4. Expectation Altering

20. Respect-ability

Respect-ability is the overall ability of a leader to convey respect and confidence in the members of the organization. A lowly respectable leader tends to have little respect and confidence in the membership's potential. A highly respectable leader has a great deal of respect and confidence in the membership. It might be noted that both the lowly respectable and highly respectable leaders tend to be accurate.

One way of assessing one's willingness and ableness to respect the membership is through the Leader's Respect-ability Scale. Take a few seconds and assess your current feelings about the membership.

Leader's respect-ability scale

1. Do I sometimes do other people's work because I basically believe that they would mess it up if I left it to them?

YES _____ NO _____

2. Do I enlist my peoples' involvement in making decisions on ways to achieve the organizational goals?

YES _____   NO _____

3. Do I delegate responsibilities confidently to my people, believing that they can do it?

YES _____   NO _____

4. Do I constantly communicate to my superiors or believe myself that I need more competent people to achieve what is expected of me as manager?

YES _____   NO _____

5. Do I allow some freedom and independence in the way my employees go about tackling their tasks?

YES _____   NO _____

6. Do I believe that the employee who is frequently late has within himself or herself the ability to somehow or other find a way to be on time?

YES _____   NO _____

7. Do I believe that the uncooperative, resistant employee can become a cooperative, involved team member with a determined effort on my part?

YES _____   NO _____

8. Do I believe that my least productive employee has more ability than he or she has shown?

YES _____   NO _____

9. Do I believe that my lowest producing employee can produce more?

YES _____   NO _____

10. Do I believe that I can correct and discipline that employee in a way that the employee can take it, understand it, and become a productive employee?

YES _____   NO _____

Now, score your answers for the number of R (Respect Responses). If some questions were not relevant for you, just add one point to your score for each one.

1. No	6. Yes
2. Yes	7. Yes
3. Yes	8. Yes
4. No	9. Yes
5. Yes	10. Yes

1-3 Low Respect

4-6 Average Respect

7-8 High Respect

9-10 Strong Respect in your employees

Analyze your ten responses and jot in a plan to improve your Respect-ability if you would like.

21. Delegating

Delegating grew out of the writings of Robert Townsend, author of *Up the Organization.* Townsend made a convincing case that decisions and responsibilities in any organization should be made at the lowest possible level. Sometimes decisions like "How many pencils should we order?" are made at a level too high, consuming time that could be used elsewhere. Townsend suggested studying your organization to find the lowest possible level that decisions could effectively be made. If that level needs additional training, provide it—smart economics.

In this book on motivation delegating is advocated for an additional reason—delegating implies respect for someone else's abilities. True, it involves a risk at first but over the long haul it helps people grow into more of a part of the total operation. As one great delegator said, "I would like my people to know everything I know so that I can move on to new issues." That person, Gene Wilkins, was vice-president of a Pennsylvania college and when he delegated he gave additional credit. His secretary signed the letter sent out to applicants in her name—not his. She was an involved part of the Student Services Department.

One of the greatest delegators I ever met was a Vancouver, B.C. psychologist. Edna Nash was past president of the North American Society for Adlerian Psychology. As local president years later, she had responsibilities to enlist help to conduct conventions. At the same time she had a private practice in psychology. Edna ran one of the smoothest conventions and after congratulating some of the responsible participants I asked them where they got their experience at facilitating conventions.

"Oh, I had never done anything like this before," one proud woman responded. "You see, I went to talk to Edna about some changes I was going through in life and I was becoming increasingly apathetic. Edna told me we could talk later about that but she had a job for me—to help conduct this convention. I panicked, explaining I could never. She insisted and here it is."

Edna Nash knew how being given responsibility can really benefit a person. Edna delegated. Delegating involves analyzing the people in your organization to see who would be capable of taking on higher level responsibilities, training them, encouraging them, and then celebrating their achievements with them.

List your personnel. Do an asset analysis on each (see ch. 4). After looking at each person's assets, what additional responsibilities do you think they could take on if you delegated them?

_____

_____

_____

_____

_____

22. "Can" Opening

When the leader hears the words, "I can't" (especially after delegating) it is a clue that the leader needs to help the person grow by overcoming the "can't"—so the leader becomes a "can" opener. "Can" opening is a leadership approach designed to create a winning feeling in a person by showing the person that he or she is much more capable than previously thought. The leader points out that most *can'ts* are not accurate, people really mean "right now I can't"—not "I could never." And of course in our past we had times when we felt, "I can't walk," "I can't drive," "I can't dance," "I can't speak in public," "I can't read," or "I can't write."

Most can'ts have some common elements:

1. Each statement is an echo of an individual's current self-image, for example, "I can't speak in public" is a personal belief based on a past conclusion and an attempt to make conclusions of the past fit into the future.

2. Each self-image statement is inaccurate, that is, it can be disproved. As you look closely at some can'ts, "I can't walk," "I can't read," even "I can't quit smoking," you will see that each conclusion could be challenged.

3. Although each self-image statement is inaccurate, the speaker is not consciously aware that the comment is inaccurate and proceeds through life as if the pronouncement was carved in his or her behavioral granite. The opinion of self is treated by the person as if it were a fact.

4. Each self-image *can't* statement limits the individual's potential achievements. As long as the person believes this personal opinion to be a fact, for that exact period of time no growth can occur.

5. With the help of a leader using the "can" opening approach the individual can see that
(a) He or she drew a false conclusion about his or her potential based upon experience of the past.

(b) Because this person couldn't do it before doesn't mean he or she won't be able to do it tomorrow.

(c) There were responsibilities when this person started in the organization that they thought they couldn't handle (before and aftering).

(d) They have a choice—continue to believe "I can't" which will lead to no attempt—result: nothing, no growth—or to believe "I can" ("can" opening) and proceed to make it happen. When making mistakes, like taking a first step, simply correct them—result: Growth.

The "can" opening leader actually enhances the self-image of individuals and propels them to greater achievements. The winning feeling is created every time a person sees himself, or herself growing.

With which individual could you use "can" opening? How could you proceed?

_____

_____

23. Expectation Altering

William Glasser, author of *Reality Therapy*, had an interesting perspective on human behavior. Glasser's views that "people are responsible" and "one person's behavior influences another's action" have influenced the ideas of management with encouragement (see Ch. 2, The 5 insights).

Glasser would communicate his respect for people by being intolerant of irresponsible behaviors. While many psychiatrists would analyze the catatonic patients who stand quietly with arms rigidly at their sides, Glasser would tell them that he expected them to be able to stand normally and talk with him. He would point out how out of place they currently looked and that they could control it. Instead of accepting their irresponsible behavior, he altered his expectations of them—and told them. He expected them to act responsibly.

Expectation altering is an approach to change peoples' unproductivity by altering, in the leader's own mind what the leader expects and then communicating the altered expectation.

The leader, as Glasser does, treats the person as if he or she can improve. "I believe in you" is a feeling that flows from leader to discouraged person. In this new vision the leader brings across these feelings:

"You are quite a capable person. I will treat you in the light of my new positive expectation. You can do it."

USING EXPECTATION ALTERING TO CREATE A WINNING FEELING

Use expectation altering with your discouraged people to bring out the best in your people. Here is one way of making this concept practical in your organization.

First, identify a few people who are marginally discouraged, for example, lacking confidence, unproductive, irresponsible, late, impolite with customers, and so on. List the specific behavior or attitude that the employee is exhibiting.

Discouraged employee	Behavior, attitude
Jo-Ann (typist-secretary)	Irresponsible (no—not specific enough.) More specifically, she rarely meets deadlines and spends too much time speaking with the other employees.

After identifying the very specific signs of discouragement present in the employee, bring into the encouraging arena the ideas discussed in the previous chapters of this book.

1. Understand and live in Jo-Ann's world for a few minutes. Do an I to you transfer and think about some of Jo-Ann's pressures, frustrations, needs, and goals. (Ch. 3)

2. List some of Jo-Ann's strengths, assets, and resources (Ch. 4).

3. It is now time to do an expectation alteration. Literally see, in your mind's eye, Jo-Ann as having the characteristics within her potential to be a responsible deadline-meeting person.

4. Schedule a special talk with Jo-Ann to convey your new expectation of her. You are now prepared to make a dramatic change in an employee's behavior in just a few minutes.

When Jo-Ann arrives, start by showing her how you understand her world, for example, "I guess there are times, Jo-Ann, when you feel as though I put a lot of pressure on you to meet deadlines (transferring). It's probably frustrating for you (peeking). I know that deadlines are frustrating for me." Brainstorm about the pressures on you and the implication of missing deadlines (exposing).

Next, share some of the assets, strengths, and resources that you have observed in Jo-Ann. "Well Jo-Ann, you are one of the most talented typists I have ever seen. And your work is flawless. You are a real asset to the company."

Now, convey your new expectations. "Jo-Ann, I feel you're the kind of person who can take charge of the situation and meet the deadlines. You've done it many, many times. I will work extra hard myself to give you more time for completing the typing on projects. By using our combined skills and understanding, together we can do it."

Now, the very important part. It is vital that you recognize Jo-Ann the next few times she successfully reaches her deadline and notice her achievement. You have just helped develop a claim-to-fame and a new asset—all because of your positive expectations! Jo-Ann becomes a winner!

How could you make use of expectation altering in your organization?

_____

_____

_____

_____

_____

24. Changing Spotlights

A teacher's expectations influence student performance. A psychologist's expectations influence client outcome. A doctor's prognosis influences the patient's progress. And a leader's expectations influence the member's losing or winning feelings.

When a member asks the question, "what does the leadership of this organization think of me?" one of the ways of answering that question is to assess "How much responsibility has the leadership given me?" It is indeed a fact that the toughest challenges are often given to the same people. Positive expectations then are communicated to a few. Some get the winning feeling over and over again.

Changing spotlights involves communicating positive expectations by taking a risk and giving the challenging job to a previously overlooked member. What a way of communicating "I believe in you!"

A new territory opened up for a small southern-based insurance company. The sales manager had to make a decision as to who would be given the opportunity to sell in the area. In making his decision he realized that he had always neglected giving Charlie additional responsibilities, which was a message to Charlie that the sales manager didn't have a lot of faith in him.

The sales manager took a risk and changed spotlights. He called Charlie in and shared with Charlie his newfound confidence (expectation alteration). "Charlie, I'd like to give you a real challenge because I feel you have the potential, with a little development, to make it big in that region. I'm handing over to you the responsibilities there. Let's see you go out and sign them up."

Dumbfounded at first, Charlie was soon on a high. Somebody finally believed in him. He immediately went out and bought himself a new suit, perhaps reflecting his new self-image. Charlie caught the winning feeling when his leader put the spotlight on him.

Who could use a little more spotlighting?

How could you give this person the winning feeling by spotlighting him or her?

_____

_____

_____

Confront with Class

The word *confrontation* in itself generates all sorts of emotional reactions in people. To some, *confrontation* elicits reminders of past encounters like the Kennedy–Kruschev missile crisis confrontations of 1962. To others the word *confrontation* triggers pictures of the likes of an unflinching Sergeant Carter shaking his index finger at an innocent Gomer Pyle. Still to others, the word *confrontation* invites positive feelings of past victories over opponents, the I.R.S. or the nasty neighbor. None of these views, neither from the victim's nor the victor's perspective are relevant for this chapter. A whole new view of confronting your employee, your children, your parents, or your organizational member will be used. The term employed from this new view is a *classy confrontation*.

A classy confrontation is one in which the leader confronts someone for the purpose of building (like a school class). The leader wants to educate, not defeat. Classy confrontations are designed to create a positive, healthy balance that is best for everyone involved. Learn to feel comfortable with and even enjoy the concept of confrontation. Confrontation, like asset focusing in Chapter 4, involves building people.

Again unfortunately, confrontation has been associated with "gut-level talk," or screaming, or firings on the spot. There are instances where the confronter would explode at the victim, attempting to destroy or retaliate publicly or privately. The victim would naturally become defensive and either retaliate directly, passive-aggressively, or would be wiped out personally. In most cases the defensiveness resulted in a message being distorted because of high emotional interchange. Here are some examples.

Confronter says, "You and I must have a face-to-face talk."

Confrontee hears, "I'm going to talk to you and you're going to listen."

Confronter says, "I'm going to level with you."

Confrontee hears, "I'm going to level you."

Confronter says, "I'm going to call them as I see them."

Confrontee hears, "You're in trouble."

Confronter says, "You just better cooperate."

Confrontee hears, "Cooperate means she tells me what to do and then I must do it."

In each instance, the confronter's words interfere with open communication and set a stage that creates an anxious defensiveness. Each of these confrontations lacks class. They are not designed to build but rather to frighten or to release anger. Consider a few of the different goals or motives of destructive versus classy confrontation:

Destructive reasons to confront	Classy confrontations
1. Trapping the other person	1. *Gathering* the facts
2. Assuming guilty until proven innocent	2. *Openness* to the confrontee's view
3. Gaining one-upsmanship	3. *Balancing* the needs of all members
4. Releasing one's anger	4. *Educating* person to more appropriate behavior
5. Instilling fear	5. *Informing* person why behavior was unacceptable

Destructive reasons to confront	Classy confrontations
6. Showing the other person "who's boss" (If one has to do things just to show who's boss that person isn't the boss)	6. *Building* the person to change behaviors in the future

REMEMBER: Confrontations have received bad press in the past because they traditionally have been associated with having destructive intent. Classy confrontations are designed to create a positive healthy balance that is best for everyone. Classy confrontations build, educate, and inform. Confrontation can be an additional leadership tool if it is given with respect for both the other and oneself (picking people up without stooping down). Confrontation is built on the principle that dealing with a problem is almost always more effective than allowing the problem to continue.

When is action called for? A man is living with symptoms of a disease, and each day he feels that the symptoms are becoming more pronounced. He is too anxious to go to the doctor for fear of hearing the worst. He doesn't realize that perhaps the problem could be treated. And maybe he has no problem at all and is living in unneccessary tension.

The biggest problem that the man experiences is his anxiety created by not knowing. His decision to avoid action on the problem drains his psychic energies. Action in this case is clearly called for because dealing with a problem is almost always more effective than allowing the problem to continue. Going to the doctor, like confronting when one is feeling ill-at-ease, is a positive action that gathers the facts, educates, informs, and builds from that point.

Many unfortunate consequences could result when a leader avoids dealing with a problem. The leader forfeits an opportunity to help someone and creates an atmosphere that may affect overall morale, and when the leader avoids the inevitable, he or she experiences frustration, anxiety, and maybe loss of self-esteem.

Negative Consequences
of Avoiding Confrontation

FORFEITING THE OPPORTUNITY
TO HELP ANOTHER PERSON

Chapter 4 stressed the important responsibility that a leader has to build people. As you may recall the point was made that one doesn't build by tearing down. It might be added that a leader doesn't build by allowing unproductive, unmotivated, or irresponsible behavior to continue either. Confrontations are a form of assistance. Remember:

- The unproductive person is not fulfilled and needs assistance.

- The irresponsible, constantly late person is not motivated enough to be on time and needs assistance.

- The person who resists change in a growing organization is threatened and needs assistance.

- The person who is in a capacity above his or her potential is not eager to go to work in the morning, and is tense and needs assistance.

- The volunteer whose responsibility it was to reach certain campaign goals and is falling far short doesn't want to constantly make excuses and needs assistance.

Assistance by a motivating leader is called a "classy confrontation." When a leader avoids confronting, the leader surrenders the opportunity to help the person to learn some new ideas that could be helpful for a lifetime.

For example, a classy confrontation can help a competent person who has only one problem, for example, poor hygiene habits, to become a more productive person. Would you not want to be confronted in this instance?

A classy confrontation can stimulate the rude waiter or waitress into new behaviors that could potentially create many more tips. Would you not want to experience a classy confrontation if you were him or her? Remember—not a destructive confrontation but a classy one!

So, one consequence of avoiding a confrontation when it is indicated is that the opportunity to help another person is forfeited. A second consequence of avoiding a confrontation can be seen on the other members of the organization.

LOSS OF RESPECT FOR LEADERSHIP OR LOW MORALE*

One fact is clear: the members of an organization see irresponsibility in one of their co-workers even before the leader does. And they are watching for the response of leadership. When leadership avoids confrontation, the other more responsible members can't help but make a note of that. "Why should we work so hard if so-and-so comes in late," and so on. "I wouldn't put up with that if I were the boss. That just makes more work for us when he doesn't pull his fair share."

A classy confrontation is one that is designed to create a positive, healthy balance that is best for everyone involved. When a member of the organization isn't pulling his or her fair share an imbalance exists, and everyone else is affected. Unless the leader is willing to give everyone else the same leeway, the imbalance will affect the membership's morale. The irresponsible party in a classy confrontation is simply being asked to give what is expected—no more, no less. The leader has not only the right, but the responsibility to confront. Avoiding the helpful confrontation may result in loss of respect for leadership and problems of lowered morale. Remember, dealing with a problem is almost always better than allowing the problem to continue.

*Obviously any area dealing with discipline or confrontation in this book needs to be tailored to be consistent with specific union contracts and specific ethical practices of any organization.

A third consequence of avoiding a confrontation impacts directly on the leader's emotional life. Timid leaders may find themselves experiencing any of the following symptoms:

1. *Passive-aggressiveness:* Passive-aggressive behavior is seen in people who have difficulty expressing feelings such as anger, hurt, and resentment. While holding those feelings in, they show an outward facade that conveys the opposite. They may smile while saying, "No, there's no problem." The leader who is upset but avoids confrontation denies the need for a confrontation and exhibits the anger in passive ways—for example, refusal to talk, putting obstacles in the way, and indirectly getting back at the target person. Passive-aggressiveness is seen in almost any relationship where a timid person feels afraid to confront.

2. *Anxiety:* Another symptom often observed in leaders who avoid confrontations is an anxiety characterized by feelings of tenseness, worries over an impending catastrophe, loss of sleep over what could happen the next day, or a continued reliving of the previous day and how situations were handled. The anxious leader has difficulties taking a stance, and making decisions as well.

3. *Displaced hostility:* When a leader avoids a confrontation with someone the "held-in" resentment sometimes reappears on an alternate target person. The computer shop manager who avoids confronting his irresponsible employees lashes out at his wife or children at home. The anger is displaced onto a scapegoat or a safer person. The tension in the organization is taken home, producing a tense home life.

4. *Escapism:* The leader who avoids a confrontation may resort to extreme forms of avoidance and denial by escaping into gambling, drugs, alcohol, daydreaming, or excessive sleep.

These symptoms could have been avoided if the leader had taken charge and confronted at the appropriate time. Dealing with a problem is almost always easier than allowing a problem to continue.

Confronting with Class: Picking People Up Without Stooping Down

Confronting, if done with the motive to educate, is a positive and effective leadership tool. Avoiding a confrontation when indicated has many negative consequences. It is clear. The effectiveness of a confrontation depends on how it is done. In this chapter several approaches are listed to help a leader 1. to set a stage upfront to prevent problems before they occur; and 2. to confront in a positive way to build the confrontee.

Confronting with class is especially relevant for the following challenges:

1. Irresponsibility
2. Discipline problems
3. First conference as a new leader
4. Lateness
5. Lying
6. Poor work performance
7. Negativism
8. Firing
9. Creating mutual expectations
10. Dealing with defensiveness

Four classy confrontation approaches
1. Speed limiting
2. Asserting
3. Disciplining
4. De-hiring

Speed Limiting

Imagine a small township police department operating without any stated laws. There are no speed limit signs

118

posted publicly, even though the chief of police has the limit in his mind. The chief tells the police officers to stop people if they are going too fast. A person driving through town is apprehended for going 60 MPH and is brought to the chief.

"But I didn't see any speed limit signs, Chief, and I just assumed that there were no limits."

"Don't be so stupid," says the chief, "common sense tells you that when you are in a town you don't speed."

"That's common sense to you. But common sense to me is that if there are no other cars on the road, no people walking down the streets, and no speed limit signs posted and I'm late for a meeting I go as fast as is reasonable."

"But what you were doing can certainly not be called reasonable."

"But with respect, Chief, what is reasonable? Where is the guideline? How can I be in violation of a rule that doesn't exist?"

"You should have known better."

The chief's failure to post speed limits was an injustice to the healthy citizens who wanted to comply but didn't know what to comply with. Lack of speed limits produces anxiety amongst the membership who wonder, "How fast can I go here," "Am I going too fast or not fast enough." Speed limits reduce anxiety by providing guidelines for acceptable and unacceptable behavior. Speed Limiting is a leadership approach designed to achieve two results:

1. to define limits to bring maximum freedom to the total membership and

2. to reduce anxiety by providing guidelines that create mutual expectations.

SPEED LIMITING GIVES MAXIMUM FREEDOM TO THE TOTAL MEMBERSHIP

Speed Limiting has the effect of expanding freedom, not constricting it. If a meeting is to begin promptly at nine o'clock with the total membership involved and one out of ten members arrives late, holding up the other nine, 90 percent of the membership lose freedom because they lost some time.

When the printing department, one out of five departments in the organization did not meet its deadline on promotional materials, the other 80 percent of the organization lost some of its freedom to act because of its dependency on the one cog in the wheel.

If one member of the tour bus took too much time at a particular scene the whole group lost its freedom and right to see the next scene, Old Faithful erupting.

Speed limits are created to maximize the freedoms of the total membership.

SPEED LIMITING REDUCES ANXIETY BY PROVIDING GUIDELINES THAT CREATE MUTUAL EXPECTATIONS

Without direction people in organizations have to guess what is expected. This guessing produces haphazard behaviors. In some instances people may feel that they are acting consistently with leadership's expectations only to find themselves confronted at some later point for poor performances.

A good friend of mine was appointed superintendent of schools in a large city in a northeastern U.S. school district. The new leader was a teacher-oriented manager who believed that teachers were the very backbone of the school, and consequently teachers should play a major role in the educational decisions. The new superintendent saw the role of school principals as encouragers to their faculty members.

The youthful superintendent's management position was in direct contradiction to his predecessor's philosophy. The previous leader believed that teachers should be monitored more closely for the sake of weeding out incompetency amongst the tutors. These changes in expectations from the top literally led to a new view of what an "effective performance" was. Be a school principal, experiencing, for a while, a confusion over establishing job priorities.

The superintendent shared, "Shortly after I took over the new position, a school principal asked for a meeting with me. The principal came to tell me, quite proudly, that he had accumulated enough facts on a few of his teachers to take action against them for the purpose of having them removed. The principal went on to say that he had spent many hours gathering information to prove these teachers incompetent." The superintendent went on, "And while I'm not naive to the fact that in teaching, as in all professions, there are incompetent people, spending 50 percent of one's important time as a principal to look for incompetence isn't justified when there are so many more important things to do."

The principal was not a bad person but he was simply doing his job consistent with what he thought was expected of him. The problem was not a complex one. The principal just needed to know what new expectations were being placed on him.

When the superintendent wisely took some time, developed and stated his management philosophy to the school principals, he initiated structure by listing his expectations and his view of an acceptable performance. His stated philosophy gave the principals the frame of reference they needed.

Do your employees know exactly what is expected of them? Do your employees know what is acceptable and what is an unacceptable performance? Do your employees know very clearly and very specifically what they are responsible for? Are your employees fully aware of the authority they have when you are and are not present? Do your employees know what kinds of decisions they can make?

While sitting with the owner of a restaurant in Edmonton, Alberta, both of us overheard a customer at the next table complain about the excessive amount of gristle on her steak. The waitress, speechless for a moment and fully aware of her boss at the next table, replied, "Sorry, I hope it's better next time." Having made a decision not to take the meat back and then save the restaurant money, she turned to her boss, Frank, in anticipation of his approval of her decision.

Frank excused himself for leaving our table and kindly advised the waitress to very graciously order the customer a new steak.

As Frank returned to the table where I was seated, he told me something that has always stuck with me.

"You can't blame the waitress for her decision not to take the food back," the highly successful restaurateur concluded. "It's my fault. As I think of it, I've never really put into words to my waiters and waitresses that my prime concern is satisfied customers." He thoughtfully continued, "The waitress thought she was making the decision I wanted her to make. And I do believe, for the most part, employees want to do what their manager wants. But not specifically spelling out to my people what I expect or want from them, not stating my needs is like trying to hitchhike without putting your thumb up. I can't expect someone to pick me up if I don't tell them I need a lift. I can't expect my employees to reach into my head and make the decisions I want them to without stating my wants."

Frank and I took a few minutes and brainstormed a simple clear-cut management philosophy, a speed limiting plan that we called a problem-prevention plan. Read Frank's Plan and consider developing a Problem Prevention Plan of your own to let your people know what you stand for, and what is expected of them.

PROBLEM PREVENTION MANAGEMENT PLAN IN FRANK'S RESTAURANT

1. I believe that above all else, customer satisfaction is the goal of our restaurant. As waiters and waitresses, constantly think of yourself, what does this customer need to be satisfied and to have a good experience while here?

2. I believe that the employees working here are as creative and important as the owner or manager. I welcome any ideas or suggestions for the improvement that any employees have. I will reward your ideas if we use them, and even if they aren't used I would be thrilled to hear them. After all, the waiters, and waitresses are out there with the customers every day and know as much as anyone.

3. I value competence, excellence, promptness, and people with a desire to improve themselves. Thus, if any of you would like to learn more about the restaurant business, I will support opportunities for you to grow by becoming more involved in the business or getting additional training in bookkeeping, cooking, and so on. Just let me know of your interests. With good employees our business will expand, which in turn will give expanded opportunities for everyone who chooses to stay with us.

4. Our restaurant faces a lot of pressures. As the owner I have made investments of time, money, and energy to build up the business. I made decisions along the way to hire certain employees who I believed would best help the business to succeed. For the most part I am pleased with employee performance. At times, however, employee behavior will make me act to get our restaurant back on course. These are problems to me:

a. When employees are late, it puts stress on the other employees to work extra hard. This is unfair and so no lateness can be tolerated. If an unexpected problem occurs, it is vital that you call us immediately so that we can replace you during that day. If an employee is late once without calling in, I will meet with the person to remind them once. The second lateness will be followed by two days off work and a third lateness will result in dismissal. I feel that it is reasonable to expect a phone call from a late employee.

b. Another behavior that simply can't be tolerated in a restaurant offering a relaxing dining experience is a negative attitude with customers or with each other. I have a customer evaluation card that will help us evaluate ourselves and our services. This is for your benefit, not mine. This will help you to receive feedback about how people view you and is, I believe, an excellent tool for a person who wants to become the best he or she can. If I hear a complaint, I will share it with you. If I begin to hear complaints regularly, for instance, more than three in one week, I will schedule a meeting with you and ask you to take additional customer relations training. A good attitude by everyone helps everyone else and let's strive to avoid problems of negative attitudes.

5. My door is always open to any of you when you have a problem or a need. I hope that your door will be open for me as well when I have a need for you to stay a little later when an unexpected big party arrives, and so on. Let's work together, avoiding small talk and negative thinking. Encourage each other and we will have a pleasant experience together. Thank you.

Frank shared these ideas at every meeting with his employees. He posted his philosophy at various locations around the restaurant as well. Because of his little extra effort, he created a harmony of expectations. He reduced many employee problems by helping his employees know what he expected of them and what he defined a good job to be.

ADVANTAGES OF CREATING SPEED LIMITS WITH THE INVOLVEMENT OF THE TOTAL MEMBERSHIP

Since most of the members benefit by a problem prevention plan or a speed limit, more and more organizations create the plan with everyone involved. Based on the Cahn Principal, "people need to be involved with decisions that affect their lives" speed limits can be developed most effectively by those who are affected by the limits.

As a consultant to an upper New York school district, we discussed how some of the problems of classroom disruptiveness could be avoided.

"It involves only two or three percent of our kids here," the high school principal commented. "The balance of our kids want to learn."

"Well, it sounds like you have a natural answer here. If 98 percent of your students want an organized classroom why not let them play a role in developing the rules that affect their lives? Instead of the administration shoving rules down the throats of everyone from their perspective, why not have rules established by the total student body. It will be a lesson in democracy and a responsibility-building experience, and it comes from them, not you."

Dialogues took place in all of the classrooms and the students created their own code of acceptable behavior

124

and consequences of violation. The administration was totally satisfied and 98 percent of the students gained more freedom through setting their own speed limits.

Fred Popejoy, vice-president of operations of a Hawaiian based insurance firm argues that leadership is quite simple if the leader is sure that the people know the answers to these four questions:

- What am I responsible for?
- What kind of authority do I have?
- What kind of decision can I make?
- What does my job entail?

How can you make use of the first approach to classy confrontation—speed limiting?

_____

_____

_____

_____

26. Asserting

When someone stands on your foot you can continue to allow the person to dig in while you seethe inside (timid); you can push the person away, throw him or her on the ground, and tread on his or her face (aggressive); or you can say, "take your foot off of my foot" (assertive).

When someone violates the speed limits of your organization you can ignore the infringement (timid), you can nail the person to the cross (aggressive), or you can deal appropriately to educate, inform, and discipline to build (assert).

Assertiveness was one of the most discussed topics amongst the behavioral scientists of the 1970s and continues to remain a topic of relevance, especially in leadership. The book *Your Perfect Right* by Robert Alberti and Michael Emmons was, in my estimation, the first practical writing on the topic. (Impact, 1982). Alberti and Emmons classified behavior into timid, assertive, and aggressive (1970), later into non-assertive, assertive, and aggressive (1982).

Asserting: Finding the balance between timidity and aggressiveness.

"I literally feared walking into my own business," the former owner of a small music shop told me.

"My young employees held me hostage in my own store. I was too frightened to ask them to do even the routine chores like unloading a shipment of new cassettes. So I did it myself. If I saw the cashier loafing while there was a line of customers waiting to be checked out, I would run over to the register and personally check each customer out. Then at the end of the day in the evening, I'd be so angry at myself for not showing my people who was boss. Here I was, the owner, the one who made the financial investment for the business in the first place, and I felt like the low man on the totem pole."

The prematurely graying, former entrepreneur continued, "Then one day it happened, the most embarrassing moment of my life. While I was running back and forth in the store like a miner in a landslide, and two of my employees were plugging into headsets, doin' their own thing, I guess, a customer looked at me and said, 'I've never in my life seen a circus like this place. You seem to be the only one who does any work around here. In fact, I've been here a number of times and every time I was here it was the same story. You were working five times as hard as all those other clowns put together. Let me do you a favor,' the customer confided. 'I'd like to talk to your manager here to tell him what goes on when he's not around and also tell him that if he should ever decide to let you go, I'd hire you immediately. You see, I own the book store in the mall and could sure use someone like you. What time will your manager be in?'

"Scared to admit that I was supposed to be the ringleader and was responsible for all of this chaos, I lied to the helpful gentleman and said that the manager was on vacation. He left. All boiled up, I immediately closed the shop and took my people to the woodshed. Giving way to my month of pent up anger, I exploded like Mount Saint Helen and fired two of my three people on the spot. And even though I enjoyed the business of selling records, within three months I had closed up shop and went to work for someone else where I wouldn't have to deal with people problems. You see," the compromised man concluded, "I'm not the kind of person who is cut out to be a manager of people."

The record store manager had irresponsible employees, but they were not quite as irresponsible as their manager was! The employees' jobs included unloading records and cashing people out; they failed. The manager's job included showing his employees what their jobs were, motivating them to achieve those goals, rewarding them when they did, and confronting them when they didn't. The manager failed as well.

The manager discouraged his employees by not giving them direction. Timid managers run away from employee problems and wish or pray that the next day they come to work the problems will magically have left; they rarely do. Perhaps you'd like to stop at this time and think about a few instances where you are timid.

On the other hand, some leaders are aggressive. While the timid leader's philosophy of life is "die and let live," the aggressive leader believes "live and let die." Alberti and Emmons write:

> *The person who carries a desire for self-expression to the extreme of aggressive behavior accomplishes goals at the expense of others. Although frequently self-enhancing and expressive of feelings in the situation, aggressive behavior hurts other people in the process by making choices for them and by minimizing their worth.*
> *Aggressive behavior commonly results in a put-down of the receiver. Rights denied, the receiver feels hurt, defensive and humiliated. His or her goals in the situation, of course, are not achieved. Aggressive behavior may achieve the sender's goals, but may also generate bitterness and frustration which may later return as vengeance. (1982, pp. 6-7)*

The aggressive leader wants not only a fair share but more than what is reasonable, or two eyes for an eye and two teeth for a tooth. Actions of aggressive leaders reflect not only the demand for justice but also retaliation, greed, or one-upsmanship.

List any circumstances where you may have crossed the line into aggressiveness.

_____

_____

_____

_____

Assertive leadership is a balance between timid and aggressive leadership. Contrast the three styles of leadership shown on page 129.

Identify a few instances where you are currently asserting yourself appropriately.

_____

_____

_____

Make a plan to become assertive in those circumstances that you have previously identified where you were either timid or aggressive.

_____

_____

_____

_____

27. Disciplining

By using speed limiting and a positive prevention plan a leader can create conditions that will lower the need for classy confrontations. When problems do still occur, the next step is to assess if and when assertiveness is appropriate. If the leader concludes that it is time to act, the approach is all important. In this approach of disciplining a very specific process to deal assertively is listed. The

Timid	Assertive	Aggressive
Die and let live.	Live and let live.	Live and let die.
I'll tolerate violation of the speed limits in the membership. Maybe someday they'll appreciate me.	I'm not obsessed with looking for violations. Most of my energies are spent on spotting what's right. However, when a violation occurs I will deal with it constructively to build the person. I will apply the appropriate discipline that is called for. Then we will start over again fresh.	I'll make the punishment so severe that no one will ever dare break a rule. I'll show them.
Avoidance, passive aggressiveness, martyrism	Private, asserting, rational thinking, active openness	Sarcasm, public disgracing, put-down

leader, of course, must use wisdom and discretion, and must tailor to the unique circumstances of others.

Disciplining with class is a five-step process, to deal with offenders of the speed limits set up in the organization. These are:

1. Gathering the facts
2. Setting discipline conference goals prior to the meeting
3. Scheduling the discipline conference
4. Using a ten step approach to confront with class during the conference
5. Following up after the conference

GATHERING THE FACTS

Some leaders find themselves with egg on their face by forgetting the simple rule of justice that "People are innocent until proven guilty." More times than not leadership lacks the full story at the onset and responds impulsively to what so-and-so said. Before scheduling the conference it is vital that a leader asks, "Is the probability strong that there was a violation of the speed limit that it is necessary to confront?" If "yes" is the answer the time is appropriate to establish goals for the conference.

SETTING DISCIPLINE CONFERENCE GOALS
PRIOR TO THE MEETING

Quite frequently leaders creat problems for themselves because they either fail to establish or forget their goals before the actual discipline meeting. Flinging through this important session without a plan guarantees the goals won't be reached. The goals govern the meeting and one should never stray from them. Here are some examples of goals that a motivating leader might establish with Charlie, a saleman who filed expense reports stating he called on a few accounts. A manager received calls from the accounts who said that Charlie had never visited them, however:

Goals for conference—Charles M.
1. Inform Charlie that I am aware of his actions.
2. Apply appropriate discipline as stated in the speed limiting and positive prevention plan or violation of policy.
3. State acceptable behavior in the future.
4. Reestablish a positive working relationship with Charlie and motivate him.

The leader gathered the facts and established the goals for the discipline conference. He was now ready to schedule the conference (Step 3).

SCHEDULING THE DISCIPLINE CONFERENCE

The ideal discipline conference is one that achieves the goals and builds the violating member. To maximize the effectiveness of the conference it is important to create conditions such that the confronted person arrives with, as much as possible, an open, nondefensive attitude.

A few suggestions to achieve the best mood for the conference include:

1. Confront as soon as you have gathered the facts and established the goals for the meeting. The longer the time between the violation and the discipline the less effective the discipline.

2. Avoid the ambiguous statement, "I'll see you in my office after work today," which has the person on edge all day. Instead try to make the time between the desired meeting and the announcement as short as possible.

3. Give the person an idea of what issue the conference will address. "Charlie, I'd like to talk with you as soon as possible about some of your expense reports so that we can straighten the matter out."

The leader has now gathered the facts, set the conference goals, scheduled the conference and is now ready for the most delicate moment a leader faces—the actual discipline conference.

USE THESE 10 STEPS TO CONFRONT WITH CLASS DURING THE CONFERENCE.

The motivating leader maximizes the effectiveness of the conference by employing these ten steps to confront with class.

1. Start the conference on a positive note. Look again at Chapter 4 to identify some of the person's assets, strengths, or resources.

"Charlie, first of all I'd like to say to you what I've often said before. You really are a great salesman. You know how to talk with people. Dale Carnegie could have learned some things from you. And you are a real asset to this company. We need you."

2. Point out specifically the problem (Avoid anger, name calling, etc.)

"It's because of your talent that I feel isn't being used to its fullest potential that I called you in here today. When your sales drop, the company sales drop. Very frankly, Charlie, I had three calls in the last two weeks from different accounts saying that you didn't call on them. Yet I have your expense reports filled out showing that you did make these calls."

3. Encourage the person to speak and listen for the person's view, feelings, and defenses (Ch.3).
"Can you tell me a little more about this, Charlie?"
Note here that defensive people must defend. The motivating leader does not let anger or revenge get lost in the defensiveness and understands it without compromising the goals. Some typical defensive reactions might include:

Defense	*The motivating leader's reaction*
1. Charlie: "You have the wrong story, boss."	1. Being open to hear the other story.

132

2. "I needed the money, etc." (pity me)	2. Understand the difficult economic times he or she faces, but keep goals in mind.
3. "I'm sorry."	3. "Charlie, it's encouraging to hear that you recognize a mistake that you made. That's great news for our working relationship in the future." (Keep goals in mind)
4. "None of the other people get disciplined" or "I'm the best, I deserve a little more." (Excusing, blaming)	4. Understand, "It doesn't seem fair to you but you know the rules, Charlie, and you violated a rule."

4. Convey your understanding and respect for the employee's view and feelings (Ch.3).

"You feel ..."

5. Present your view and why the employee's actions presented a problem to the organization.

"I filed a report to my boss about the number of calls our salespeople made last week. My report is now inaccurate. Also, the accounts are angry that they are not being serviced. These are two problems that are associated with your actions, Charlie."

6. Indicate the discipline along with a clear understanding of what the discipline will be if the violation occurs again.

7. Share very clearly the desirable behavior you now expect.

8. Point out again the specific assets, strengths, and resources the individual has.

9. Provide hope and confidence in the employee's ability to come back on the team. Mark a new beginning.

10. Thank the employee for his or her time.

The motivating leader controls the conference by using the Ten steps of confronting with class and is now ready for the last phase of the discipline process, the follow-up.

FOLLOW UP THE DISCIPLINE CONFERENCE

Charlie's manager was sensitive to any improved behavior in the new Charlie. He made it a point to be the first to say, "Good job! Your work sure is an asset to our company, I'm proud of you, Charlie."

An assertive, encouraging leader who confronts with class can turn even the most troublesome into producers by the using the five phases of effective discipline:

1. Gathering the facts

2. Setting discipline conference goals prior to the meeting

3. Scheduling the discipline conference

4. Using the ten step approach to confront with class during the conference, and

5. Following up the conference

While it is fresh in your mind make a few notes to remember the most important aspects of disciplining as it relates to you.

_____

_____

_____

28. De-hiring

De-hiring is a term developed by my close friend, author Donald Scoleri. It is based on the realistic fact that there are times when the organization's needs and the member's needs are not compatible. Let's assume that the organization has made reasonable attempts to understand (Ch. 3), to build (Ch. 4), and to give meaning (Ch.5) and concludes the marriage is good for neither. When a member's needs are not being met, he or she looks for alternatives—thus de-hiring the organization. There are times as well when the organization's needs aren't being met by an individual and thus the organization needs to de-hire. In either case, the experience of a person de-hiring the organization or the organization de-hiring the individual can be anything from painful to relieving. How it is done makes the vital difference.

Facts to remember when de-hiring

1. Chances are the person is neither happy nor fulfilled in the organization.

2. Chances are that the person senses that the event is going to occur.

3. Chances are the person subconsciously wants out anyway.

4. Chances are he or she has had a discipline conference.

5. Chances are that the member is having social problems in the organization with other peers.

The motivating leader who de-hires with class is well aware that needs of the individuals or the organization are not being met. This demands a response of assertiveness on the leader's part. The leader is also aware that the person is probably dissatisfied and unfulfilled in the current situation.

A few things that the motivating leader keeps in mind when de-hiring are:

- I've communicated to this person a sincere analysis of his or her assets and resources with even some advice as to where he or she more effectively fits.
- I haven't destroyed this person out of my own anger or retaliation needs.
- I've honestly listened to this person's side to understand and am still convinced that de-hiring is appropriate.
- In cases where it is relevant I've pointed out how the economy of the company or other reasons for cutbacks necessi-

tated the decision and not his own or her own personal worth.

- This decision, while temporarily appearing to be to his or her disadvantage may, in the long haul, work out for this person's best.

If you are currently in the process of de-hiring, how can you make use of any of these approaches to de-hire?

_____

_____

_____

_____

Ten crucial things to remember
Ten practical things to do from chapter 7
Confronting with class

1. Remember: Dealing with a problem is almost always better than allowing the problem to continue, so **Do:** Become determined to address those problems that are monopolizing a lot of your mind space. But first, make sure

1. Your expectations are clearly stated
2. You are prepared to confront based on the phases of confronting with encouragement in Chapter 7.

2. Remember: Two ineffective styles of leadership that produce disharmony are timidity, in which confrontation is avoided, and aggressiveness, in which the leader creates unnecessary confrontation, so **Do:** Find the balance between the timid and the aggressive style. Be an assertive, encouraging leader. Make it crystal clear with your people that you will confront when there is a violation of rules and expectations, but by the same token you are not living over their shoulders just waiting to spring on them.

3. Remember: Many problems are related to the simple fact that the leader has not clarified what the membership roles, responsibilities, and rights are, so

Do: Ask yourself if your people know the answer to these four questions:

1. What am I responsible for?
2. What kind of authority do I have?
3. What sort of decisions can I make?
4. What does my job entail?

4. Remember: You and your membership need to have mutual understandings of what their job entails and what is acceptable and what is unacceptable behavior, so

Do: Over the next few weeks, develop your philosophy or Problem Prevention Plan which sets speed limits. This plan will

1. Give guidelines or standards
2. Reduce anxiety
3. Demonstrate that everyone is bound by the same rules
4. Enable your people to see the consequences of violating the rules
5. Give you peace of mind
6. Maximize freedom for most.

5. Remember: When you must meet with a specific person to confront over lack of performance or a violation of Speed Limits, there are two ways of proceeding; the destructive or the constructive way, so

Do: Become familiar with the five-phase process of discipline

1. Gather the facts
2. Set conference goals
3. Schedule the meeting
4. Use the ten steps to confront with class
5. Follow-up

By using these five phases you can enhance the chances of having a constructive discipline conference to steer the person back on track.

6. Remember: Unless you have specific constructive goals for your meeting you have no directions, no target to shoot for, and you may wander aimlessly in this important encounter, so
Do: Know exactly what you want to achieve in your meeting. Make sure the conference is not designed for simply the enhancement of your own ego or releasing your anger or revenge. A constructive conference is designed to develop more appropriate and productive behaviors or attitudes.

7. Remember: Assume that when you confront someone he or she will naturally, become defensive, so
Do: Be prepared to cope with defenses to your confrontations by being familiar with the leader reaction list to defenses on pages 132–33.

8. Remember: An effective discipline conference deals with specific behaviors or attitudes (not personalities), and give specific suggestions for improvement, so
Do: Make sure the person knows specifically why he or she is being disciplined and the specific behaviors that are expected in the future.

9. Remember: A positive beginning opens the person up to what is to follow. By ending your conference on a positive note you invite the person back on the team, so
Do: Make the discipline conference mark a new beginning with no grudges held.

10. Remember: If a person is dissatisfied, he or she leaves or de-hires the organization. If an organization is dissatisfied, it de-hires the person. But de-hiring need not be a destructive experience done without class, so
Do: Build the individual by identifying those assets that you see in him or her and point out where he or she might be more fulfilled.

Put Your People in Second Gear

The ultimate test of what a leader is really made of is not during the sunny times when a boom allows wasted resources to go unnoticed. The ultimate test of a leader's substance is when the dark clouds descend upon the organization and every voice is too busy singing doom songs to build an ark. It is in these times that one or two people emerge to face the rain head-on and make plans for the future knowing they have the resources to make the sun come out tomorrow. These people are the opti-realistic leaders. This chapter takes a microscopic view of the mental workings of these rare individuals who make the difference in the success of an organization.

It was in the summer of '82 and the economic tornado of the times was savagely folding many businesses, leaving its autograph in the form of bankruptcies and unemployment. The artists of the TV, radio, and news media were painting pictures that reflected further and deeper doom. It was a time when optimistic arguments were received as well as bikinis in church. Yes, many businesses, especially the housing and automobile industries, were closing their doors.

But, many didn't. Some industry weathered the destructive storms as they watched their neighbors and competitors drown in the economic winds. And I was fortunate enough to be consulting with one such north-

139

eastern U.S. chassis building company. There I observed the power of opti-realistic leadership. The leaders made a commitment to dig deeper into the ideas and spirits of their people to create a sunny future for the company.

The president of the company expressed his far-thinking philosophy in a session with his management group, "These are the most challenging of times and with the right attitude we can find new ways of facing these new challenges." The humble optimistic leader put his people into second gear; the vice-president of sales, a sensitive young man, made a commitment to additional training of the people in sales. "Our sales force really needs motivation as well as techniques to help our clients become more optimistic." (This was a contrary position to many businesses who, out of fear, were spending less on training.) The vice-president of engineering, inspired by the optimistic leader, made a commitment to dig deeper into the customer's new needs and develop products that distributors couldn't resist. (This, as well, was a contrary position to that taken by many companies who responded out of fear and reduced their product lines.) The vice-president of finance made a commitment to explore alternative ways for distributors to pay for their purchases. And while I could go on and on giving examples of how the president of this company put his people into second gear during the tough time when many leaders were prophesying doom, I don't believe it necessary. Some of this company's competition were closing down. Through optimistic and realistic leadership, this company was preparing for expansion. The difference between an organization making it or not when coping with a challenge is often the result of the attitude of leadership.

The Opti-Realistic Leader

Tough times in an organization are as inevitable as rain. Doomsday leaders can be observed responding to the crisis like a building looking at the swinging construction ball, awaiting the demise. Other pessimistic leaders help-lessly fold during the storm and aren't heard from again

140

until the sun shines. On the other hand, quixotic leaders act as if it weren't raining and then get drenched because of their refusal to face reality.

The doomsday and pessimistic leaders breed a "what's the use" philosophy amongst the membership. And when people are functioning out of the belief that there are no answers they make no attempt to seek them. On the contrary, the overidealistic leader doesn't encourage a search for the solution to the problems because he or she doesn't acknowledge the problems. Hence, the overidealistic leader's style breeds distrust or disrespect since he or she is viewed as either dishonest or naive.

And then there emerges the one leader in ten. This is the person who sees the problem, faces it clearly and realistically and communicates an optimism that says, "We can find a solution." This person, the opti-realistic leader is one of the first people contacted for help from top leadership during a crisis. This leader is not a game player, but a solid citizen, solid with strength, solid with hope, and a stranger to excuse making. It is the opti-realistic (OR) leader who has school buildings and streets bearing his or her name.

What is it that separates the OR leader from the other 90 percent? It is, first of all, an attitude and a strong conviction to see reality "as it is"—undeluded by personal needs. Secondly, the OR leader has an underlying belief that there are solutions to the problems that the organization faces.

In this chapter a number of approaches are listed that the opti-realistic leader can take to ignite the energies of the membership to solve these problems:

1. Frustration
2. Burn-out
3. Cynicism
4. Unmotivated
5. Stagnation

Six second-gearing approaches
1. Jonas Salking
2. Environmental Engineering

3. Talking it up
4. Sweet surrendering
5. Rational leading
6. Opti-realistic leading

29. Jonas Salking

If you think of it, there was a time only a few decades ago when there were no washing machines, airplanes, buses, satellites, geodesic domes, Mcdonalds, Wendys, Burger Kings, open-heart surgery, trivial pursuit, cabbage patch dolls, TV, and almost everything else that you see around you. And if those few decades ago the world was composed of only pessimists, today there would still be none of these!

These modern day conveniences exist only because of optimists whose minds could see beyond what their eyes saw. Perhaps the best example is Jonas Salk who discovered the vaccine that cured polio. Suppose Salk had been a pessimist and had given up on his journey. Suppose he had listened to the cynics of the day and turned his energies elsewhere—like writing about despair and hopelessness in life. Fortunately for the world he didn't. He described in his book *Survival of the Wisest* that we should not be limited in our visions of the future by our experiences of the past. (Salk, 1973)

"Jonas Salking" is a leadership approach designed to create the feeling in the membership that "our problems do have solutions." This mental attitude orchestrated by a second-gearing leader helps push the membership's mind one step further. A frustrated membership sees no options. And as Baruch Spinoza the philosopher wrote, "For as long as a person believes a task to be impossible for that exact period of time no progress is possible." But the hour, the minute, the second that someone inspires others to find the solution, that is the moment that the membership moves toward fulfillment. Henry Ford said, "Believe you can or believe you can't, either way you'll be correct."

More conservatively I'd like to add that those who are inspired by a leader to look for the answer to the challenge may or may not find it, while those who don't look at all will not find it. And I like maybes better than nos.

Jonas Salking can be achieved in a variety of ways. Here is one possible approach:

1. The leader identifies past examples in the organization—when everyone was ready to give up, someone discovered a solution and the organization solved its problem.

2. The leader encourages everyone to relax, to plant in their minds the conviction that this particular problem has a solution somewhere.

3. The membership brainstorms about possible solutions in an atmosphere of acceptance.

4. Every attempt is noticed and recognized, (especially if some of the membership laughs at a suggestion).

5. The leader responds enthusiastically to any progress with "We're getting closer—the answer is there, let's find it."

6. Celebrating the progress. "Look at how far we have come tonight with your suggestions."

How can you make use of Jonas Salking in your organization?

_____

_____

_____

30. Environmental Engineering

B.F. Skinner, the brilliant developer of Behavioral Psychology, has noted that people are products of their environments. To that I would like to add that environments are products of people. Motivating leaders take responsibility to shape the environment which will shape the attitude of the membership.

Yes, just as the air we breath in from our physical environment affects our physical health, our psychological environment affects our psychological health. An unstimulating, drab or negative environment is not likely to lead to second-gearing. Motivating leaders build uplifting, positive environments by being environmental engineers. Some factors that a leader can alter are the:

1. People environment
2. Physical environment

ENVIRONMENTAL ENGINEERING: PEOPLE ENVIRONMENT

To keep oneself in second gear it is crucial to avoid—as much as possible—people who are down on life. People's attitudes rub off and the rule of social influence is that we tend to become like the people with whom we associate.

The motivating leader knows that I must surround myself with people who have the characteristics that I myself want to develop. If I want to learn Spanish I am better off spending time in Spain than in Canada. If I want to quit smoking I must surround myself with non-smokers and if I want to appreciate life I must surround myself with people whose ideas on life will influence me positively.

A motivating leader also realizes the principle that you never seek advice from someone who has not achieved the things you want to achieve. Don't ask a depressed person for the meaning of life. Don't ask an angry person for his or her secret. Don't ask a bankrupt person how to invest.

In *Think Your Way to Success* I suggested that the reader hire a board of positive consultants to help design his or her environment:

Don't take on such an important challenge as designing your environment by yourself. As director of Environmental Engineering, you have the power to not only de-hire, but to hire people to assist you. So hire your own board of free advisors to be part of your super successfully stimulating environment.

The simplest task in the world is selecting the people who will be on your board of positive consultants. Identify at least five people based on these qualifications: 1. You feel positive about yourself and life when you are with them; 2. You feel courageously willing to try new experiences and take new risks when you are with them; and 3. You feel free to speak and share even your craziest new ideas in their presence. Please take this important exercise to heart. Jot down the names of the people you have honored by your selections. In your environment, a positive friend is like a rare gem.

When you have established who you would like on your board of advisors make a point of telling each of them that you have read a book on the importance of having positive consultants. Tell each of these people the three requirements for a person to be a positive advisor and that you have selected him or her for the position. Then ask each of the group to consider accepting a position on your advisory board and express your confidence in the fact that acceptance involves nothing more than continuing to be himself or herself. I'm sure your comments will elate all of them to no end. How would you feel if someone complimented you by saying that out of everyone he or she knew, you were one of the most positive influences on his or her life? After you share your news, you will rarely find any one of these people "down" in your presence.

Become determined to spend more time with each of your board members in the future. Make more plans to see them and talk with them, even if only on the telephone. When you consider the fact that people pay $60 to $125 an hour to talk with their psychiatrist or to listen to motivation lecturers, friends who help a person feel positive are worth quite a lot. Don't neglect positive advisors, the richest sources of input.

And the great news is that even if you can't be near your board of advisors because of distance or timing, it doesn't matter. When facing a difficult decision or a challenging situation, recall your advisors' thinking by visualizing their reactions to the event. In your imagination, confront each positive person with the situation and picture each one's response and advice. You will find the results of their advice to be quite interesting, if not incredible. Most of your free advisors will probably agree on the best course of action for you! As director of Environmental Engineering for yourself, hire the most positive people you know and watch your positive self-image grow. Now, add an honorary board of advisors composed of the most inspirational thinkers in the world. (1982, pp. 116–117).

The first way to engineer your environment is to let your thinking be influenced by people's ideas that work. A second way to influence your environment is to alter its physical components.

ENVIRONMENTAL ENGINEERING: PHYSICAL

A second-gearing environment is one that gives the membership a constant pep talk, reminds them to keep plugging away, and provides for the needs of relaxation, stimulation, meditation, and inspiration. Advertisers spend millions annually on jingles, phrases, colors, sights, and sounds that will most effectively influence buying habits. Why? Because it works. And creating a stimulating, second-gearing environment can work for an organization if a leader takes advantage of this multi-million dollar idea.

Many companies take their work force to a fine hotel for their training and development programs to get them away from the ho-hum everyday work atmosphere. They realize that if you want new ideas, you need a new surrounding to stimulate the membership.

1. *Start an advertising campaign in your environment.*
Imagine you are the leader of a weight loss group. Encourage the membership to build their environments at home and work around the theme of weight loss. Take the goals of "I want to lose twenty pounds," for example. Encourage your people to get up an environmental engineering plan and include as many stimulating ideas and reminders as you can.

146

Put up a sign on your refrigerator which reads "No High Calorie Foods Permitted in This Area."

Add a few pictures of trim people around this sign on your refrigerator. Buy a scale and weigh yourself the same time each day—record it. Tape up your desired magic weight number at various conspicuous points in your house.

Assign a special "my exercise room."

Leave some environmental reminders like "You Can Do It" to inspire you to go that extra pound.

Carry with you a calorie book and jot down the estimated calories on everything you eat—even the one potato chip.

Reward yourself with, not a super dessert, but a brand new outfit that will compliment your weight loss.

Whatever your goal is, start an advertising campaign in your environment.

2. *Put yourself on a diet of positive motivation tapes.*
Listen to inspirational speakers like Zig Zigler, Dr. Robert Schuller, Earl Nightingale, W. Clement Stone, Napoleon Hill, Doug Cox, Dr. Norman Vincent Peale and many, many others.

3. *Read only positive books.*

4. *When crossing paths with inspirational quotes, jot them down.*

5. *Listen to positive music.*
Imagine you are feeling really enthusiastic as you are driving to a meeting to inspire your membership and you hear the following imaginary songs.

What's the Use In Going On—Nothing Matters Anyway

Nothing Ventured Nothing Lost

Everybody's Out for Themselves

I May Be Paranoid, but That Doesn't Mean People Aren't After Me

You're Born, You Work Like a Dog for a Living and Then You Die

How would you feel after that experience of being barraged by negative music? Now imagine that immediately before you speak with your membership you hear these imaginary songs:

Today Will Be My Day

Born to Win

Together, New Heights

Second gear yourself and your people by putting positive music in your environment.

6. *Expose yourself to positive media.*
Put everything that you hear into perspective. After viewing a documentary on crime, we tend to get down on life. But the fact is that 99 percent plus of the North American people will never go to jail.

After we see a news story on a vandalized house in New York we tend to generalize and get down on life. But the fact of the matter is that 99.99 percent plus of the houses were not vandalized. (Can you imagine a TV anchorperson saying, "Tonight we'll have action shots of a house that wasn't looted?")

No, the focus is on the negative because it is rare. As a motivating leader don't build your philosophy of life on the rare—it's not scientifically accurate.

Expose yourself to positive media and encourage your membership to do likewise.

How can you make use of environmental engineering to second gear your membership?
Environmental Engineering: People Environment

_____

_____

_____

Environmental Engineering: Physical Environment

1. Start an advertising campaign (plan)

_____

_____

2. Put yourself on a diet of positive motivation tapes.

_____

_____

3. Read positive books (plans).

_____

_____

4. Inspirational quotes you can use (plans).

_____

_____

5. Positive media to be exposed to (plans).

_____

_____

31. Talking It Up

Albert Ellis and Robert Harper, in their now classic *A New Guide to Rational Living* (1975) unravelled the connection between what we tell ourselves and our resultant emotional adjustment. What we tell ourselves affects how we look at things, how we feel about things, and eventually our own words lead us into action (second-gearing) or inactions (immobilization). Do not depressed people have a depressing vocabulary? Do not up people have an uplifting vocabulary and tell themselves things that will propel them onward?

What we tell our membership is vital to create that winning, on the move, active second-gearing feeling. Our words are the propellants to stimulate the minds of our people up over the hills and the obstacles in the way. After reading this group of words record your feelings exactly at the moment you finish:

closed	lifeless
stale	rut
same	boring

stagnant	decayed
dead	routine
common	ho-hum

Your reactions or feelings about what the words do for you.

_____

_____

These are stale, talking-it-down words. Do they generate a down, stale feeling within you?

Now consider this group of words and record your feelings upon completion:

crisp	original
on the move	new
fresh	ascend
uplifting	virile
high	debut
youthful	prime
birth	more
bigger	

Your reactions or feelings to these words:

_____

_____

The opti-realistic leader second-gears by talking it _up._ Contrast the style of two different leaders to the same situation.

Talking it down leader	_Talking it up leader_
Things look bad.	We face an exciting challenge ahead of us.
I see you people didn't reach 20% of your goals.	Congratulations—you reached 80% of your goals.

We might as well pack it in.

Let's go that extra mile and show people what we're made of.

Maybe it can be done.

It can be done and we are the ones who can make it happen.

We're not as young as we used to be.

We will never be younger than this moment.

Our organization is too small to take that on.

The quality, not the quantity of people we have here are what makes us qualified to face that challenge.

Across the street that new restaurant is scheduled to open soon. So on their opening day we will cut back on our orders of meats and other foods. Brace yourself for a tough year.

Across the street that new restaurant is scheduled to open soon. Their advertising will bring us benefits because much more traffic will be passing our way each day. We are building a bigger sign to get noticed. We also have a real advantage because we have a well established crowd here, who after experiencing something new, will come back to us because of our quality service.

Now when you ask for money from the public, be very careful and watch what you say.

Every person you see can be a link in the chain that leads to the final cure of cancer. The more people you see the more people are given this opportunity to be a part of society's and their own future. Help them feel that with your robust thank you from one in four Americans for your contribution.

There are many ways of approaching the same challenge with your membership. One way is to use language that talks it down, giving the membership the feeling of "what's the use—we are already going as fast as we can go." The alternative approach is to second-gear them by talking it up to mobilize the organization's people resource. The difference is everything!

How can you use talking it up in your current leadership position with your people?

_____

_____

_____

_____

32. Sweet Surrendering

In opti-realistic leadership the leader uses the optimistic approaches like Jonas Salking, environmental engineering and talking it up and combines them with realistic approaches, the first of which is "sweet surrendering."

Sweet surrendering grew out of the work of my friends Bob Powers and Joanne Hahn in their article that appeared in the *Personal & Guidance Journal,* 1978, entitled "Resignation or Courage? The Wisdom to See the Difference." The two fellow Adlerians argued that courage is the willingness to change, that change can be a move toward accepting inevitabilities.

On a personal note, sweet surrendering occurs when my dear dad and I canoe through some Pennsylvania rapids, and after we do all we can to approach a rocky garden of water, we eventually have to relax and give in—surrendering only to get stronger—losing ourselves to find ourselves.

Sweet surrendering is a leadership approach that involves facing reality head-on without demanding that it be any other way than the way it is.

Devon was passed over for a major oil company pro-

152

motion. Many thought he was the fair-haired boy who was in top management's favor but the decision was made to hire someone else instead from outside the company. Devon saw this as a raw deal and unfair. So, at age 30, he became frustrated and bitter about losing the job he thought was his. His attitude that "things are unfair" and his shouts that "it's not what you know it's who you know" made Devon not only unpleasant to be around, but a person who would mentally sabotage some of the success of his new supervisor who took "his job." Devon's thousands of claims of unfairness, of organizational injustices, and negative actions soon forced him to be transferred to another division and by age 36 he was actually put into a created job that could do no harm— but, no good as well. A brillant sparkling career died an early death because of Devon's refusal to sweet surrender to reality.

Imagine how different Devon's career could have looked if he had been realistic. "I didn't get the promotion, and that's a disappointment to me, but I have a few decades of potential success ahead of me and I'll show top management what I'm made of and that I respect their decision."

When is the moment that the opti-realistic leader and the membership make a decision to sweet surrender?

Here is the question that the organization asks.

"Will our time and energies be more effectively spent with this issue or with another issue?" (Be specific about the other issue.)

If the conclusion is "yes," second-gear.

If the conclusion is "no," sweet surrender.

Are there some issues that you currently face that could benefit from a sweet surrender to free up your energies?

_____

_____

_____

_____

33. Rational Leading

In his study on the characteristics of the healthiest human beings, Abraham Maslow found that one of their ingredients was the ability to see things clearly without a need to twist, distort, or bend them. Maslow wrote:

> *One does not complain about water because it is wet or about rocks because they are hard or about trees because they are green. As the child looks out at the world with wide, uncritical eyes, simply noting and observing what is, without either arguing the matter or demanding that it be otherwise, so does the self-actualized person look on human nature in himself and others. (1954, p. 207)*

Imagine the second-gearing power a leader has when he or she helps the membership to face reality, as it is, and not as it should be (*should* as defined by them). Energies bogged down with irrational thinking are lost energies. The rational leader has a clear perspective of what the facts are and those facts are the only rational starting point.

Rational leading grew out of the genius work of Albert Ellis in *Executive Leadership: A Rational Approach (1972).* Many earlier philosophers approached the idea of rational leading, for instance, the stoic Epictetus, who 2000 years ago argued, "No human is free who is not master of his or her own thoughts" and "humans are not disturbed by things, but by the views which they take of things." Later, Marcus Aurelius wrote, "no human is happy who does not make himself so." Emmanuel Kant, the eighteenth-century philosopher exalted the power of the way we perceive things in his philosophy of phenomenology that suggests that human behavior is a function of the way people look at things (see Ch. 2, phenomenology).

The rational leader's responses to crises and challenges are effective because 1. the leader dares to see things as they are and then 2. operates harmoniously with the external world to 3. either encourage the membership to manipulate the external world or accept it (sweet surrendering). The rational leader makes every effort to wipe out the frustrating results of irrationality.

Irrationality—what is it? How can you observe it? Well, first of all, irrationality is grandiosity, an overexaggerated sense of self-importance. In *You Can Do It*, I wrote:

> *People who refuse to face the realities in their lives inevitably become frustrated. Their energies become wasted in directions that are unproductive. People who fail to accept reality suffer from a superiority complex in that they believe that the world was created to personally serve them and to protect them from injustices, frustrations and unpleasantries.*
>
> Losoncy, p. 52, 1980

Irrationality is seen when people "take personally" events in the universe, such as, the world, the economy, society, and other people. They, like the child waiting for Santa Claus to be with "only me," exaggerate self-importance. It's almost as if they believe that the sun is no longer the center of the solar system but rather they believe, "I am"; therefore things better go my way or else. Can you see how this perspective moves one away from a healthy adjustment to reality, binding up one's energies in despair, anger, or frustration?

The rational leader develops a plan to help the membership overcome or avoid three primary irrational beliefs:

1. We must be perfect in every decision we make and everything that we do, or else we must not act because if we make a mistake it would be devastating. The whole world will look at us in a condescending fashion and our very existence would be threatened. There couldn't be a tomorrow for us (notice the exaggeration present in irrational thinking).

2. People must treat us kindly, fairly, and considerately. And not only that, they must act the way *we* want them to act at all times. If they choose to act the way they want rather than the way we want, it is a personal attack on us and a sign that we are losing power and control and it is a sure clue of our impending demise. Obviously we are more important than others because we have free will and we won't allow them to have the same.

3. The universe must make things easier for us and must always make events go our way because the world revolves around us. When things don't go our way it is a sure sign that the universe is treating us as inferiors and demonstrates that forever more, not just today, things will go downhill.

Rational leading should help rid the membership of its irrational thoughts: 1. We must be perfect, 2. People must act the way we want them to, and 3. The world must be fair to us and act favorably toward us. In place of these irrational thoughts the rational leader helps the membership to face reality and develop a plan to change the crises or surmount the challenges.

Irrational thought	Rational thoughts and action
I messed up that huge order. How can I face the owner tomorrow? I think I'll quit. What an idiot I am.	I made a mistake. I'll immediately do what I can to correct it, explain my error, and tell the owner what I learned from the experience to help me the next time.
My report is due on Friday. Oh well, I have Wednesday and Thursday to get to it. Friday is a long way off.	My report is due on Friday. There is no magic that will do the report for me. I have to do it. It won't be any easier to do tomorrow. Let me do it and get it out of my way and my mind. It's up to me.
I'm late again. It's because of the traffic. The traffic should not have been this heavy today. I'll explain that to the boss.	I'll have to remember how heavy this traffic is, adjust to it, and leave earlier tomorrow. I'll offer to stay fifteen minutes later working today since I'm being

| (Whining) Look at this rain again. Why does it rain ten days in a row? | paid to work eight hours a day. |
| | It's raining, I'll use my umbrella. |

Since most people think irrationally, believing that the universe's events revolve around them, it is a formidable task for a rational leader to help people put themselves into a realistic perspective. It can be done with humor. But no matter how it's done the rational leader avoids these six irrational words:

Should

Shouldn't

Ought

Ought Not

Must

Must Not

Whenever hearing any of these irrational words, which suggest the world must comply with my *should*, the rational leader simply asks the membership to rearrange the irrational sentence with the question, "What's our plan?"

Are there any situations where the membership or yourself are having trouble accepting, "What's our plan?"

_____

_____

_____

_____

34. Opti-Realistic Leading

Most of an organization's frustration is the result of one of two basic mistakes made in its thinking. The first is the failure to face and accept reality as it is (they need sweet surrendering and rational leading in these cases).

The second basic mistake in thinking that produces frustration is the failure to realize all of the alternatives available once the organization faces and accepts reality. In this case, the organization needs Jonas Salking, environmental engineering, and talking it up.

The opti-realistic leader inspires within the membership a desire to take the best of both worlds, optimism and realism. Let's contrast four different types of leadership styles:

PESSIMISTIC

Unrealistic (PU)	*Realistic (PR)*
Mental Set: Things are terrible now and they will even get worse.	Mental Set: We're trapped. There are no answers.
Action: Runs away from reality, sees doom, lives in defense, makes excuses	Action: Faces reality but sees only the negative parts of the reality. Tends towards sameness.
Results: Carries morale downhill	Results: More of the same, living on the status quo.

OPTIMISTIC

(OU)	*(OR)*
Mental Set: "What problems?"	Mental Set:
	1. There's a problem that is a challenge to us.
	2. Somewhere there is a solution.
	3. Let's generate alternatives.
	4. Let's find the best alternative.
	5. Let's act.
	6. Evaluate action.
	7. Same process 1-6.
Action: Runs away from reality, sees no problem and	Action: Faces reality but sees the positive parts of

thus doesn't face the issue squarely	that reality, uses resources to find a solution, believes that for things to change we must do something differently.
Results: Creates a period of temporary unrealistic elation followed by a crash with reality	Results: Adjusts to challenge with new solutions.

Which leader would you want in your organization?

How could you make use of Opti-realistic Leadership in your organization?

_____

_____

_____

_____

Ten crucial things to remember
Ten practical things to do from chapter 8

1. Remember: The difference—the biggest difference—between an average leader and a superior leader is seen not during the good times, but rather during the tough times, so
Do: Thrive on crises. Love challenges as an enthused child loves a new puzzle. Convey to your people 1. the realistic facts and challenges and 2. your beliefs in their abilities to dig deeper to find a solution to the challenge. Be an opti-realistic leader.

2. Remember: Many people give up when the organization faces problems and conclude that there just aren't any solutions, so they stop looking, but the optimistic leader ignites the minds of the membership, so
Do: Inspire your people by Jonas Salking them, communicate an unbending belief that your problems have solutions and that they are the kind of people who can find them.

3. Remember: Just as the food we eat affects our bodies, the people we associate with affect our thinking, so

Do: Surround yourself with positive, uplifting, on-the-move people in your personal and professional life. Their golden ideas will rub off on you and eventually on the organization.

4. Remember: Your environment affects you—but more importantly you affect your environment, so

Do: Take charge of your environment and influence those things that influence it to keep your enthusiasm and optimism high.

5. Remember: Depressive people use depressive language. Angry people use angry language. Those who believe that a challenge is insurmountable immobilize the organization by down-talk, but motivating leaders use talking it up language, so

Do: Use talking it up by speaking in positive, lifting, upbeat language. Use up words to your people. See problems as challenges, and obstacles as opportunities to second-gear your people.

6. Remember: Sometimes your people's energies can be better spent on one challenge than another. In that case it is most appropriate to sweet surrender, so

Do: With the membership, determine the most effective way to spend energies. If the membership feels that one challenge would take an inappropriate amount of time, accept it as it is by sweet surrendering then quickly mobilize the energies to attack the next challenge.

7. Remember: Frustration is a result of your people failing to face and accept tough realities, so

Do: Be a rational leader who helps people realize that the world doesn't revolve around them. Help them to develop a more rational view of self, others, and life.

8. Remember: The highest reflection of one's unwillingness to face the world rationally is through the use of the words *should, shouldn't, must, must not,* and *ought, ought not,* so

Do: Whenever you, as leader, hear any of those six irrational words tell the person to change the sentence to answer the question, "What's my plan?"

9. Remember: Unrealistic leaders fall into two types; the pessimistic unrealist (PU) believes that things are terrible now, can only get worse, and there is no hope. The optimistic unrealist (OU) ignores the realites of the problems that lie before him or her, so
Do: See reality head-on as it is and where it is without catastrophizing or without ignoring.

10. Remember: Realistic leaders fall into categories; the pessimistic realist (PR) sees and faces parts of reality clearly with most attention on the negative, ignoring the positive resources in the organization. The glass of water is half-empty to the pessimistic realist. The second type of realistic leader is the optimistic realist (OR) who sees reality clearly but also sees hope and holds a conviction that there are solutions to the challenges, so
Do: When problems arise face them as an OR type leader—an opti-realist who puts people in second gear.

Erase Apathy and Uncooperativeness

People are not born uninvolved, disinterested or apathetic. Nor are they born rebellious or uncooperative. Anyone who has studied young children knows that the physically healthy child wants to create, to belong, and to contribute. What happened along the way to produce these discouraged symptoms of apathy, rebelliousness, uncooperativeness, closed-mindedness, and irresponsibility? In *Turning People On: How to Be an Encouraging Person*, I identified a few techniques of discouragement:

1. Discouragement through domination
2. Discouragement through insensitivity
3. Discouragement through silence

Discouragers Who Use Domination

Some dominators are well-intentioned and want to be helpful. They communicate, "I'll help you with your responsibilities since you might mess up."

A new chef was added to a restaurant and the old chef, Charles, stood over his shoulder every step along the way. "No, no, you'll kill them with all that seasoning," and "wait until I check the meat before you serve it" were just a few of the common statements of advice given by the talented old-time chef. The young cook never had a chance to learn by doing. The young chef became discouraged, feeling "This is so hard I'll never catch on," and he quit.

Unfortunately, dominators tend to get into leadership roles and sometimes squelch the ideas of many people unintentionally because of their overpowering style.

The high school football coach called all of the plays for the team; consequently when the quarterback went to college he had no experience of thinking for himself. The college coach, a builder of people (not a builder of self) couldn't break the dependency the young man had developed on his previous coach. Dominators discourage by "doing for" rather than encouraging people development.

Discouragers Who Use Insensitivity

Insensitivity can be observed when a leader acts as if he or she is better than the membership, or more important than others because of a role or title. The insensitive leader treats people as "its," or only "producers," not people. The insensitive leader is often on an ego trip and overestimates the importance of what he or she does. Frequently, the insensitive leader doesn't even know some of the names of the membership. And in most cases the insensitive leader is quick to use one-upmanship.

Betty and Larry have a family business selling home products. In one day they made twenty-three sales, a personal all time high. They couldn't wait to tell Carl, their leader, who enlisted them in the program a few weeks before. When Carl listened to the proud couple express their achievement, he cut them short by pointing out to them how he once sold not just twenty-three—but sixty in one day. Carl went on to tell them how he did it and never once congratulated them. Instead of leaving with a feeling of accomplishment, they had feelings of inferiority and defeat. "How can we ever top sixty?" Betty asked. "I

163

don't know," her exhausted husband responded. After a proud achievement both went home discouraged by an insensitive leader.

Discouragers Who Use Silence

Silence is not golden in leadership when recognition for achievement is involved. The motivating leader does not assume that people know they are doing well. Failure to communicate positives may lead to discouragement in people.

The teacher returns the test paper to the student noting, "Well, you failed two tests in a row now," rather than noting the fact that last time she failed by thirty points and this time by only three points. The teacher was silent about the progress.

The doctor takes the blood pressure of an anxious man, jots down a number on a piece of paper, and says absolutely nothing to the man about the reading. The doctor is silent about the reading.

"Why should I tell them they're doing a good job?" the steel company foreman says. "That's what they're paid for." The foreman is silent about the workers' performance.

Carolyn worked as a nurse in a midwestern state. She felt quite adequate about her job there, looking forward to going to work each day and felt as though she made quite a contribution to the hospital. Some time later, she and her husband moved to another state. With her excellent references, she quickly secured another nursing position. But after three months she resigned, saying she felt that she was no longer a competent nurse. When asked what she did differently at this hospital that made her incompetent, she replied, "I did everything the same except that no one ever said how I was doing, so I assumed I was performing poorly!" Carolyn is undecided about her career, but she has expressed an interest in areas not related to working around people. Discouragers who use silence are totally aloof to the leadership potential they have, but aren't using.

In this chapter, approaches to motivate discouraged people to contribute their ideas will be discussed. This chapter is especially relevant for dealing with these specific problems:

1. Lack of confidence
2. closed-mindedness
3. fear of change
4. irresponsibility
5. apathy
6. rebellion
7. uncooperativeness
8. power struggles

Four goal-directed approaches
1. Morale Analyzing
2. Goal-Centering
3. Performing Perfection-ectomys
4. Crediting

35. Morale Analyzing

Apathetic or uncooperative people are dispirited and the organization loses its potential. If a leader wants to assess the perceptions of people, one technique he or she can use is a morale analysis. The morale analysis is a tool to measure the members' level of identity with the organization and how valuable their contribution is.

These are a few questions that the leader can ask of the membership and then can analyze the results to develop future plans. The leader can decide whether it would be more effective to conduct the analysis anonymously or not.

1. How do you think the organization feels about your ideas?

____ I don't know, they never said.

_____ They said they were interested, but I tried to give them some ideas and I never heard anything.

_____ I think that if I offered a good idea, they would consider it.

_____ They are really interested and give you credit.

2. How do you feel the organization would handle an idea that would be an improvement but was inconsistent with its current beliefs?

_____ I don't know.

_____ They haven't listened. I tried and was put off.

_____ They would honestly listen and maybe change or would explain why they aren't using it.

_____ Other (write in please)

_____

_____

3. Who knows the most about your responsibility or job?

_____ Me

_____ Someone at my level

_____ Someone I report to

_____ Other (write in please)

_____

_____

4. Can you identify ways that would improve your effectiveness in your responsibility?

Yes _____   No _____
If Yes, what would they be?

_____

_____

5. Which do you feel is most important in your organization?

_____ Not making mistakes

_____ Creating new ideas

_____ Achieving goals

166

While no statistical analyses have been completed, the morale analysis will help the leader to see what's going on in the organization.

36. Goal Centering

Some leaders put their compass on the organization's goals; other leaders are more concerned with their own ego. Goal centering involves making decisions based upon what's best for the organization, not what's best for one's self.

The ego-centered leader believes	*The goal-centered leader believes*
My ideas must always be the ones that are used. If one of my people gives a suggestion on how to improve something it is a direct attack on me. And my ego won't allow someone to try telling me that my previous ideas are wrong. And so I'll put any new ideas in their place immediately.	It really doesn't matter whose ideas are used here. The most important thing is that the best, the most efficient, and the most enjoyable ways of doing the job are used. The source of the idea has nothing to do with the value of the idea. The goal is the best idea.

If you can identify some instances where you are ego-centered, make an alternate plan to motivate your apathetic or uncooperative people through Goal Centering.

_____

_____

_____

• It is one of the simplest rules of psychology: Only the person who feels threatened is the one who needs to defend. The manager with a poor self-image is the one who needs to defend his or her own ego at the cost of new ideas and better ways.

I saw the best example of how an ego thinker functions while serving as director of admissions and registrar of a Pennsylvania community college. The college administration established a goal of increasing its student enrollment. To meet this goal, one of my plans was to enlist the ideas of the students themselves on how they thought the best way of promoting the college might be. I selected a social psychology class. The project I gave them was entitled, "Applying the Principles of Social Psychology to Increase Student Enrollment." Put yourself in the excited students' shoes. Your very ideas could play a role in achieving a goal for your college.

My previous ideas about marketing a college were insignificant compared to the ideas that the students generated. I was so elated with their practical suggestions that I invited the dean of the school to listen to the ideas of these "turned on" students. An error in judgment on my part, to say the least! The ego-thinking dean listened to the first inspired student who suggested that we form a speaker's bureau. The student explained that the speaker's bureau could be composed of students who would go to parent-teacher meetings and to civic, social, and business groups to discuss the program that the college offered. With arms folded, the dean responded, "It'll never work. I've tried that before. You just can't get your foot in the door of these groups. Those people are looking for exciting speakers who have something to offer." The chin of the student who gave the suggestion dropped from noon to six o'clock. Put yourself in this student's shoes. You worked hard to make a contribution to achieve a goal and you were told your idea wouldn't work.

Another student exclaimed, "Then why not invite a famous speaker, someone who has something to offer, to our college and open the lecture to the public? We could have an important political figure, writer, comedian, or even singer perform here. We could advertise in the newspapers, and when people come to the program, we could pass out literature about the school." The ego-thinking dean rebuffed the idea by concluding that the college couldn't afford this idea because of the limited budget.

The dean felt threatened. Like an ego thinker, the dean thought that if someone else developed the idea to increase enrollment, it would make her less worthwhile and unneeded. When you put yourself in this student's shoes, how would you feel?

Have some fun with this one. Tap your understandings of how to motivate people and their ideas. Imagine that you are the dean of that school. Instead of being an ego thinker, be a goal thinker. Watch how you could take suggestions like those given by the two students, expand on their ideas, and reach the goal of increased enrollment. Be a goal thinker.

Consider the suggestion of the first student: "We could form a speaker's bureau composed of our own students and go out into the community to speak to a variety of groups about the programs our college offers." Now, with a totally open, Goal Thinking approach, take just two minutes to expand on that student's idea. But remember, don't get ego involved. Put red lights to your ego and green lights to your goal. Dream of the possible. Give the student credit and build on the idea.

What did you come up with in two minutes? If you came up with just one idea, you would be more effective in reaching the goal than a thirty-thousand-dollar-a-year dean—successful leadership through Goal Thinking.

The ego-centered leader believes	*The goal-centered leader believes*
If I have a personality clash with another individual in an act of revenge or punishment, I will get back at that person, even if it affects what's best for the organization.	The organization is bigger than me. And the organization's success leads to my personal success. If I have a personality clash with another person, it is vital that I be objective about that person's contributions. It would be self-centered and narrow to get my therapy here in the workplace at the cost of the lives of the organization and the other employees here.

The director of purchasing for a small Canadian oil-drilling company was traced to be the major factor responsible for the company losing its advantage over its equal-sized competitors. The ego-centered purchaser refused to deal with a salesman whose company produced a more efficient drill. Yet the competitors were purchasing the new drill, which allowed them to drill faster and cheaper.

Upon examination of the situation, the vice-president found the director of purchasing had all sorts of excuses as to why the company did not at least consider purchasing the new drill: "It'll never work for us. I don't like the idea right now—we're just too small." And then one day, the real reason came out. "And this salesman (who owned the drill franchise for this area) thinks he can walk in and out of my office without an appointment. I don't put up with that from anybody."

Imagine the vice-president's reaction! The company and all of the employees in the company were affected by one leader needing ego therapy and using his position to retaliate against another individual.

The goal-centered leader rises above individual conflicts and views people's ideas from a higher level, a more objective light.

1. Make a determined effort to listen to the ideas of all of your people regardless of whether you like or dislike them personally. It doesn't follow logically that if you dislike someone he or she then doesn't have anything to contribute.

2. Think big. Make your decisions based on what's best for the organization and the people in it. Be marked as a big thinker who doesn't need the leadership position for therapy!

37. Performing Perfection-Ectomys

The growing organization is constantly in a state of change, adopting, altering, and adjusting to the external demands, its own internal needs, and its goals. These changes are frequently resisted by people who have become comfortable with the status quo and uncomfortable with the new. In many cases, the change resistor is a

170

perfectionist who views change as a potential threat because he or she could "do it wrong" the new way.

Sometimes others suffering from "perfectionitis" are those who appear apathetic, never making contributions or giving new ideas, and those who panic when making mistakes. People who have difficulty making decisions also are saying by their actions, "I'm afraid of doing something unless I'm guaranteed ahead of time that it will be perfect." In each of these instances, change-resisting, apathy, fear of mistakes, and unwillingness to make decisions, we see evidence of the underlying disease of perfectionitis. They need a Perfection-ectomy performed by an encouraging leader.

To perform a Perfection-ectomy, a leader must sensitively go to the world of the discouraged person and experience his or her private logic. (See Ch. 2, Phenomenology) Remember, people operate out of the way they (not I) look at life. After experiencing the private logic, the leader is in a position to understand more fully where the perfectionitis is located. For example, if I offer a suggestion, like I did once before, and some of the other members laughed at it and the boss said it would never work, it can be humiliating, so I'll just keep my idea to myself.

After understanding by transferring to the member's world, the leader performs the delicate surgery by planting these new ideas in the person—to remove the perfectionism and replace it with the "courage to be imperfect."

1. No idea is wrong. All good new breakthroughs were novel ideas. At most your idea won't be usable.

2. There is not just one right way of doing things, but there are as many ways as there are people to look at a challenge.

3. You are one-of-a-kind. We need your unique input. We may not agree, but after all, if both of our ideas are the same, one of us becomes necessary.

4. The value of an idea is not based upon who gave it. The value of an idea is based upon its ability to work.

5. Some ideas have value in themselves, some ideas have value because of their ability to generate new ones.

Don't ignore sharing your idea just because it doesn't appear to have immediate value.

6. Don't wait for just the right moment to act. When a new idea appears—share it.

7. The only poor idea was the one not shared. In fact the sharing of the idea is more important than the actual content of the idea. Why? Because if a person keeps sharing new ideas a usable one will eventually emerge, but if an individual holds back because "it maybe stupid," nothing new will appear.

The sensitive Perfection-ectomy is successful when the member makes the first move to share an idea, shows a willingness to see a new way of doing things, or dares to make a decision and take full responsibility for it. Don't miss the opportunity to celebrate that moment with the person. You played a big role in his or her growth as a member ... and as a person.

How can you make use of performing a Perfection-ectomy in your organization?

_____

_____

38. Crediting

Crediting, like underwhelming in Chapter 4, is limited to a secure leader. Crediting is the process of giving open credit to the person who gave an idea. Dale Carnegie was a master at giving credit. President Ronald Reagan had a plaque on his desk that read, "No task is impossible to achieve for the man who doesn't care who gets the credit." William Ouchi, author of _Theory Z_, discovered the reason for the impressive productivity of the Japanese worker—trust. If workers give their supervisor a new idea, they trust the superviser to give them the credit.

Crediting is an effective leadership tool because it fulfills the needs for attention, recognition, and contribution. It also motivates and gives meaning because "that's my idea they are using—I will make sure it works."

Crediting even motivates some others who sense that if they share an idea with this leader my—not my supervisor's—autograph will be written on that idea.

Some leaders use crediting by assigning the name of the person who developed the idea to the idea, for example, the Johnson plan and the Pullman car.

Crediting can also be used at regular meetings whereby the leader informally or casually looks at one of the members and comments, "Jim, you have been telling me this for some time. I now understand what you are saying." Jim has been credited.

A bit of warning here—be cautious about the overuse of crediting one particular individual and overlooking the accomplishments of others (the Wayne Gretzky Syndrome). Sometimes resentments build. Also be sensitive to the results of crediting. For example, teenagers who are credited sometimes may be hassled by their peers out of jealousy. In these cases, credit in private. But don't stop crediting.

Rules to credit
1. Think of some ideas of the past and try to tie them to their source—credit them even though it was some time ago.
2. Never take credit when you can give it.
3. Remember how you felt when someone gave you credit for ideas of yours in the past. You can now, as leader, give others that same impetus.
4. To really turn someone on share with your leader, manager, or supervisor their idea with credit to them. Not only will they be planted positively when they hear about it but your leader will be impressed with your style.

Who could you give credit to tomorrow to give meaning and purpose to their efforts?

_____

_____

_____

1. Remember: Apathetic, uninvolved, rebellious, or closed-minded people are not born that way. They want to belong, contribute, and grow, but they are discouraged, so
Do: Show the apathetic person how he or she has something to contribute. Win the rebel over by letting him or her know you could really use the input, and turn closed-mindedness into openness by building pride in his or her growth.

2. Remember: Theoretically, every person has better ideas on how to improve his or her effectiveness, so
Do: Spend a few minutes with each person, the "expert on the job," and create a safe atmosphere that will help the person to think improvement.

3. Remember: A sensitive leader is "in tune" with the morale and perceptions of the membership, so
Do: Consider conducting a formal or informal analysis on how the membership feels about the way its ideas are handled. One such form is listed in this chapter, Morale Analyzing.

4. Remember: Ego-centered leaders use their position for their own therapy; goal-centered leaders use their position to achieve the organization's goals, so
Do: Keep personality out of decisions. Remember that the value of an idea is not based on who gives it—but rather on how effective the idea will be.

5. Remember: When someone criticizes you, the criticism is a potential opportunity to grow, so
Do: Be a criticism welcomer. It marks you as a leader who is looking to improve and to be the most effective leader possible. It also marks you as a model to your people so that when you confront them with class they will be able to handle it less defensively.

6. Remember: You can assess your people's growth potential by observing their openness to new ideas and their desire to improve, so
Do: Identify people who handle criticism nondefensively. They may very well be the people whom you look toward

when making decisions for future advancements. With openness there is no limit to growth potential.

7. Remember: Change resistors or people afraid of making a mistake or making decisions are suffering from perfectionitis, so
Do: Perform a Perfection-ectomy to remove fear of the new or fear of responsibility.

1. Go to their world to understand it (transfer);
2. Communicate "no idea is wrong, there are many ways of doing things. We need your unique input. The value of an idea is not based on who gives it, but on its ability to work. Some ideas have value because they trigger other ideas," and "when a new idea appears, share it."

8. Remember: When someone takes a chance and shares an idea, it is an indication that a successful perfection-ectomy was performed. The disease can reoccur, so
Do: Don't miss the opportunity to acknowledge your appreciation of the idea. Get back to the person—from the time the idea is shared he or she is waiting anxiously for your opinion. Offer thanks!

9. Remember: Some apathetic people or uncooperative people have previously shared an idea with someone, and the leader took credit. This built distrust and turned them off, so
Do: Make crediting an important and regular practice. Can you think of a recent idea you used where you could again give a credit to the originator?

10. Remember: Psychologists estimate that humans use only 5–10 percent of their creative potential, so
Do: Unleash part of the other 90 percent of your membership's ideas by slashing the fear of failure, the key mental block to creativity. Be a goal-centered leader and reinspire your apathetic and uncooperative people to be contributing team members.

Turn Individuals into Team Players

The whole is more than the sum of its parts; Team Power is more than just the sum of individual efforts.

The gravelly voiced drill instructor opened up the session at boot camp with the greenies by doing what he always did during the first workout. His goal was to establish very quickly the fact that he was the boss and that the pecking order began with him on down.

"Let me start off, right here and now, by saying that maybe some of you guys think that you are pretty tough already and don't need this training." As he looked out on to the sea of rookies, merely boys, he continued, "Now you see I'm not that big, but I'll tell you this. I can lick any one of you here. So if any of you tough ones want to show the other boys how you can whip a seasoned sergeant come up here right now and let these other boys see you eat dirt. Come on, I'll take any one of you on."

Even the breathing stopped as the young recruits sat submissively in his scope. The sergeant was so accustomed to this motionless compliance that he could let the moments hang as easily as one counts sheep. As he was ready to move on to the next phase of training, the silence was broken by a man in the next to last row.

As the recruit stood up with all of his at least 300

pounds (mostly above the waist) a pair of unblinking eyes, teeth like a baracuda's, and arms like oil pipelines, he politely blurted, "Name's Hardrock from Coal City, U.S.A., Sergeant—I'd like to take you up on your challenge."

For a moment, the drill instructor looked as nervous as Don Knotts, then he quickly transferred all of his muscles to his mind. As recruit Hardrock neared him, the drill instructor, digging for his deepest voice, asserted, "Hardrock, let me have a few words with you." The two huddled and their caucus ended with the sergeant's right arm over the boulder's shoulder. The sergeant looked out at the other recruits and asserted, stronger than before, "All right, you guys think you're big, don't ya? Well I have news for you. Hardrock here and I will take on any two of you!"

The sergeant took one giant step in understanding the importance of team power. But he stopped short. Not only enlist the cooperation of the Hardrocks over your team but help everyone be a contributing, cooperating team member. When you do, you are experiencing the potential of team power.

There are a number of reasons why Team Power is much more effective than just individual power:

1. Team power helps all people feel a part of the whole, thus satisfying each person's wants for belonging and contributing to the team (See Ch. 2 on Human Needs).

2. Team power rallies a group around a common goal. It unites many individuals by giving them common interests and common achievements to celebrate.

3. Team power instills pride in not only self but in the whole team.

4. Team power leads to greater involvement and greater understanding of each person's role and how he or she fits into the goals of the team.

5. Team power makes cooperation and mutual encouragement the call words of the day.

Since people are social beings, team power is a natural overflow and fulfills the social and belongingness needs.

In this chapter, a few approaches will be discussed on how to build a team feeling so that more of the membership will be involved and motivated. This chapter will be especially relevant for dealing with the following challenges.

1. Destructiveness and competitiveness within the membership
2. Uninvolved members
3. Backbiting
4. Cliques
5. Isolates
6. Rejected members
7. Uncooperativeness among different departments
8. Individualism

These approaches will be discussed in how to turn self-centered individuals into team players:

Five Team-Building Approaches
1. Team Theming
2. Cooperative Focusing
3. Sociograming
4. Welcome Mat Weaving
5. Team Esteeming

39. Team Theming

The motivating leaders are *we*, *our*, and *us*, not *I* or *me* thinkers, they never stray far from the emphasis on the total team. The leader has a continuous plan to get the membership to think *we* not *I* in their actions and decisions. And although this flies in the face of some of the cultural trends, "I'm better than him" or "I'm faster than her," the leader wants everybody motivated, not just one or two. How can you as leader help your people to think *us*? By an active campaign to promote the theme of team.

Initiate your own advertising campaign on team power. Talk up the importance of team power at staff meetings. Here are some tips to get your campaign rolling:

1. Build team theme by pointing out how the great athletic teams work together by using team power. Use some specific examples of teams who have or had one great athlete but didn't succeed because of lack of team cooperation. Drive home the point that no individual ever won a Super Bowl—it was a team effort.

2. Build a team theme by posting signs in the work or family environment to remind your people to think team. Just as the food you eat affects your body, the ideas around you affect your thinking. Constant reminders in the environment can help nourish team power thoughts, For example:

- Think team
- Does someone need a boost today?
- Give credit
- We are superbowlers
- Everyone here is a teammate
- Cooperate

Be creative and add your own relevant messages to the work environment to constantly remind your people to think team.

3. Think team theme in all of your decisions. Be sensitive as to how your decisions affect all team members. By constantly giving your toughest challenges to the same person, are you unwittingly creating a one-man band? By constantly acknowledging only one department, are you ignoring a few others, relegating them to feeling like "subs" rather than as necessary contributors to the team efforts? Think team in all of your decisions.

So build team theme by thinking *we, our,* and *us* in everything you as leader do.

What other ideas could you use to bring about a team theme?

_____

_____

_____

40. Cooperative Focusing

The encouraging leader who sees team accentuates an atmosphere of allies. When you see an organization with flaring spirit and strong morale, you will find a talented leader behind the scenes. And no doubt, one of the approaches the leader uses is an *emphasis on cooperation* and a de-emphasis on competition among team members.

Focusing on cooperation to build team power is a shift from the past, when a leader would play one person against another. And while competition is a crucial fact of life, your company or organization is competing against other companies—competition in your own department discourages more people than it motivates. A competitive atmosphere is the antithesis of an atmosphere that builds team power.

Do you remember when in school you had a teacher who emphasized competition and gave the top student the first seat, the second best the second seat, and so on? When some students received recognition, what were the attitudes of the students sitting in the last half of the classroom? Some of the by-products of heightening competition among your teammates include:

1. Claims of injustice, unfairness, and favoritism.
2. Blaming—the test was stupid, the teacher (manager) doesn't care.
3. Excuses—if only it wasn't for ....

Team power cannot happen when competition is stressed.

Emphasize cooperation by putting an accent on the times you observed cooperative behaviors. A friend of mine, Dr. Don M., made a commitment to tap the potential of team power. Dr. M., a divisional vice-president of a major U.S. based steel company, is one of the top metallurgists in the world. But besides that, Don was a leader who placed a great deal of energy in helping his five unique departments work together.

While addressing his 400 employees on the concept of team power, I was inspired by Don's opening remarks. Like clockwork, the doctor of metallurgy showed an acute knowledge of human behavior when he recommended, "Look at the power we have when we work together." He cited five specific instances in which cooperation among the five divisions achieved specific results. Don helped 400 highly intelligent men and women to continue working together by taking a few minutes to encourage team power by emphasizing cooperation as opposed to competition. He told the following story on the power of working together.

A person was given the opportunity to observe the differences between heaven and hell. The person was first taken to hell. There he observed a large banquet hall of delicious foods, yet no one could eat because their arms were extended straight out and they could not be bent to put the food into their mouths. "The frustration of hell," he thought. "You can see the things you can't have. You are immobilized."

The observer was then taken to heaven, and, to his amazement, he observed the same delicious food and the same unbending arms. But here, in heaven, the people had figured out a way to eat. With their stiff arms, they faced each other and fed each other. Cooperation was the difference. Cooperation helps people achieve their goals.

Craig D., the manager of a highly successful Mexican family restaurant in Maui, Hawaii is a real leader who knows how to tap the potential of team power. While dining at the restaurant one evening I was fascinated by the ways the maitre'd, the cocktail waitress and even the entree waiter and dessert waitress worked together as harmoniously as a fine melody. In the course of one meal we experienced four different people serving us. And each person's arrival at the table was deliciously timed. Having been so intrigued by this team harmony I asked one of the waiters how this atmosphere came to be.

"Oh, Mr. D. loves employees to have the family feeling with each other. He gives us pep talks on being a family. In fact this month he set up a goal of selling a certain number of desserts, and said if we achieve that goal, he will take us all out to dinner!"

It is so much more effective when the team members are working together rather than competing against each other. Craig D. knew it. Emphasize cooperation and turn individuals into team players. How can you use cooperative focusing as a leader?

_____

_____

_____

41. Sociograming

A sociogram is an interesting approach that a leader can use to gain information about the social structure of the membership, which will assist in building a greater team feeling. Sociograming grew out of the work of educators who desired to understand their children in the classroom better. Through a sociogram, the teacher could gather information about class leaders, isolates, mutual friends, mutual enemies, and so on, and could then develop a strategy to develop a more harmonious classroom.

How does a leader do a sociogram? First the leader makes a decision either to actually ask the membership about its choice or non-choice of people to work with or hypothesize what the membership's would be if asked. The advantage of asking is perhaps that some of the responses would be more accurate. The disadvantage of asking is that the leader may feel uncomfortable.

There are two questions that the leader asks or imagines asking of each of the membership.

1. If you were to work on a group project, who would you choose to work with? (positive choice)

2. If you were going to work on a group project is there someone that you choose not to work with? (negative choice)

The leader then plots the responses like this:

Name	Positive choice	Negative choice
John	Joe	Jesse
Joe	John	No choice
Jesse	Joe	John
Bob	Joe	Jesse
Tom	John	Bob
Lee	Joe	Bob
Merle	Joe	Bob

Next the leader constructs a sociogram by putting all of the member's names in circles. An unbroken line with an arrow is drawn from the chooser to the person who is a positive choice. Then a broken line is drawn from the chooser to the person who is the negative choice.

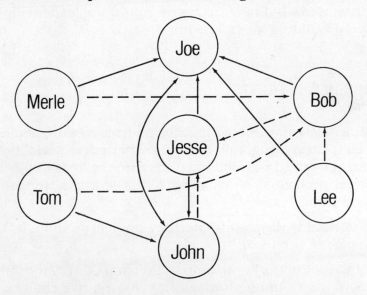

The sociogram reveals the following:

1. Who is/are the leader(s)? The leader is the most frequently chosen employee (unbroken line). For example, Joe was selected by five people.

183

2. Who is/are the most rejected employee(s)? The most rejected person is the one who receives the most negative choices (broken lines), Bob, for instance.

3. Are there any isolates in the sociogram? Isolates are the people who were neither positive or negative choices of anyone.

For example, Merle, Lee, and Tom are isolates.

4. Are there any mutual positive choices? Joe and John, for example.

5. Are there any mutual negative choices? John and Jesse, for instance.

6. Are there any subteams? For example, two leaders who have a following, creating two factions that could lead to a competitive disharmony in the organization. There are none here.

OK, the leader now has some valuable information to help analyze the patterns that exist within the membership. What are some potential insights that the leader might gather, and what new strategies might the leader employ toward building a team feeling?

POSSIBLE INSIGHTS

A. Bob may not feel as though he is a team member. In fact, if anything, Bob perhaps experiences social problems at work. (Does Bob have absentee or drug or alcohol related problems? If so, maybe this is a clue to understand him.)

B. Merle, Lee, and Tom may not feel as though they are part of the team.

C. Joe is the key to help build team power since he is sought after, and he himself has no negative choices.

D. John and Jesse would be a twosome who may particularly need some extra thought.

E. Is it possible that John and Jesse are competing for Joe's attention since they both chose Joe and rejected

184

each other? Could there be jealousies present? (If so, imagine the devastating cost of heightening the competition between John and Jesse.)

These are just a few hypotheses that would need to be further supported by the leader's observations. Suppose you were the leader of this group and you believed your sociogram and personal observations to be relatively accurate. Imagine that you needed to assign people to work together in groups of three, two, and two. Outline a strategy to produce hamonious groups and to maximize membership to the team.

Group A	Group B	Group C
_____	_____	_____
_____	_____	_____
_____	_____	_____

42. Welcome Mat Weaving

The motivating leader can weave a welcome mat for new members, welcoming them on the team or can extend a welcome back mat for vacationing or disciplined members.

Team power can be built by helping new members who splash into the potentially cold workplace feel to be accepted members of the team. Here are some suggestions.

1. Prepare the old-timers for the new person by encouraging empathy towards the rookie. "Joan, we have a new receptionist starting tomorrow. Her name is Linda and she has a pretty good background in the areas of ..., that I know are areas of interest to you. Would you please take a few minutes to help her feel comfortable with the others here? Sam, you lived in the midwest. Tomorrow we have a new girl starting here as receptionist, Linda. She's from Hutchinson, Kansas. Maybe you can help her feel comfortable by initiating some common experiences."

2. Build team power by helping the new people to see who the other cast of characters are and how their work responsibilities intertwine.

3. Empathize with the new person's feelings by doing an I-to-You transfer with the first-day employee.

4. Help people returning from vacation to feel that their efforts were missed.

5. Build total team power by bringing the disciplined person back on the team and encouraging the other people to do so as well.

Build team power by being sensitive to your people's needs to feel a part of the team. Jot down any instance in the oncoming weeks where you could employ welcome mat weaving with your people.

_____

_____

_____

43. Team-Esteeming

No one doubts the importance for an individual to have positive self-esteem. Positive self-esteem gives confidence and is the source of creativity and productivity.

It is just as important for an individual to have positive self-esteem as it is for team members to feel positive team-esteem.

Team-esteem is built by an asset-focusing leader who rallies around the resources, achievements, and the uniquenesses of the membership.

1. Rallying Around the Resources of the Team

- Build team esteem by frequently pointing out all of the vast resources the total membership has.
- Build team esteem by enthusiastically sharing how each person's resources fit into the total team's resources.

- Build team esteem by demonstrating your positive expectations of your people because of their vast resources.

2. Rallying Around the Achievements of the Team

- Lift team esteem by never failing to celebrate achievements.

- Build team esteem by showing how far the team has come in its achievements (before and aftering).

- Elevate team esteem by dreaming and imagining with them about future achievements.

3. Rallying Around the Uniqueness of the Team

- Show how this team is special and unique by identifying those qualities that this team has that others don't.

- Identify team's claims-to-fame about special skills and talents that this unique team has.

- Build team esteem by creating nicknames or mottos that relect a uniqueness, for example, "the Whiz Kids," "the Fighting Irish."

Ten crucial things to remember
Ten practical things to do from chapter 10

1. Remember: One of the most basic human wants is to belong and contribute to a greater whole than oneself, so
Do: Think about each of your people to assess the degree to which his or her needs to belong and contribute are satisfied at work. The ones whom you conclude are not getting their wants satisfied are those who need your intervention to become part of the team.

2. Remember: Many people are inclined to think "me" rather than "team" in their actions, and it becomes the responsibility of the leader to develop a plan to change their mental sets to "we," so
Do: Initiate an active team power campaign. Talk up the team at your staff meetings. Fill the environment with reminders to everyone to think team and to work together.

3. Remember: When you heighten the natural competition that already exists among your people you create more losers than winners. It is a natural psychological process that losers must defend themselves through blaming, making excuses, or claiming that the winner "got the breaks." Build team power by encouraging cooperation and discouraging competition among your people, so

Do: Analyze your every day "way of being" with your people. Are there times when you play one person against another? If so, be sensitive to finding ways to encourage cooperation among your people.

4. Remember: While many leaders make the mistake of believing the way you motivate people is through highlighting competition, the motivating leader knows that highlighting cooperation is a more effective approach to develop all of the people, so

Do: Point out cooperative behavior whenever you see it, for instance, one person sharing knowledge, helping, supporting, or encouraging another. Soon the membership will realize what the leader values. Be a cooperative focuser.

5. Remember: By creating a team theme as opposed to an individual theme, the leader brings in more of the resources of the organization, so

Do: Bring in the out, lift up the down and help everyone to be contributing team members by team theming everything you do.

6. Remember: To build team power, it helps to understand the social structure of your people. One of the most effective tools a leader can use to achieve this is a sociogram, so

Do: Construct a sociogram to help identify the leader, the rejectee, the isolates, mutual friends, and mutual enemies to help you develop strategies to help everyone to be an involved, contributing member of the team.

7. Remember: In the hustle and bustle of your challenges as a leader it is easy to overlook the feelings of a new person thrown into a new organization for the first time, so

Do: Be sensitive to a new person and have a plan to help the person's first day anxieties be minimized. Weave a welcome mat for new members.

8. Remember: After a person is disciplined or returns from a period of time away they may feel alienated from the team, so
Do: Have a plan to welcome people back, making them feel a member of the team again.

9. Remember: Self-esteem is important, so is team-esteem, so
Do: As leader of a team build pride through rallying around the team resources, achievements, and uniquenesses.

10. Remember: Most successful teams are not composed of individuals, but instead have people who work together, so
Do: Make team a regular part of your vocabulary and help everyone feel the pride of that winning touchdown run by one person, blocked by ten others, and supported and encouraged by the rest of the team.

Practical Applications

Motivating Leadership Applied to Specific Situations

Listed below are a few common challenges that the motivating leader faces in the development of a strategy to motivate. They are on the left. On the right are the numbers of some suggested approaches to refer to when building your motivation plan. This section is designed to help the busy leader quickly get his or her hands on some practical ideas without having to page through the entire book. Remember, though, that your own creativity is as important as the ideas on these pages, so create your plan in conjunction with these approaches.

Absenteeism	9, 10, 15, 23, 25, 26, 40
Alcohol problems	2, 11, 15, 23, 25–27, 38
Alienated people	1, 6, 9–11, 15–17, 19, 31
Attention seekers	Ch. 2, see charts.25, 26, 39, 40, 41
Apathy	9–12, 16–19, 24, 35–38, 41
Boredom	9–13, 16–19, 21, 24, 29
Burned-out members	1, 3, 9, 11, 13, 16, 17, 24
Closed-mindedness	1, 5, 10, 21, 24, 30, 35, 37, 40

Chronic discipline problems	1, 10, 15, 25–28, 30, 40
Communication problems	1, 3, 4–6, 39–41, 43
Complaints of being Overwhelmed	1, 5, 29–31, 34
Cynicism	1, 3, 5, 24, 25, 35, 37, 38, 41
Disrespect	3, 9, 10, 20–24, 41
Distrust	1, 3, 5, 14, 23, 38
Dominators	Ch. 2, see charts.1, 5, 25, 26, 30, 36, 38, 41
Drug problems	1, 2, 11, 15, 23, 25–27
Defensiveness	3, 4, 9–11, 17, 30, 31, 35, 38, 40, 41
Egoism	3, 25, 26, 36, 39–41, 43
Feelings of insignificance	1, 6, 9–14, 16–19, 24, 41
Firings	35, 26–28
Interdepartmental conflicts	1–6, 30, 39–41, 43
Irresponsibility	5, 7–11, 17, 20, 23–26, 35, 41
Lack of meaning	1, 6, 9–14, 16–19, 24, 41
Lateness	5, 7, 9, 11, 13–17, 19, 23, 24, 35, 41
Low self-esteem	1, 6–19, 21–23, 30
Lying	Ch. 2, see charts.3, 25–27
Misunderstandings	1, 3–6, 30, 39–41, 43
Marginal performers	3, 7, 9–11, 13, 14, 17, 19, 20–25, 41
Overperfectionism	33, 34, 37
Power struggles	Ch. 2, see charts.1, 3–6, 9, 20, 26, 35, 36, 39, 40
Scapegoats	1, 6, 9–18, 21, 22, 24, 30, 41
Self-centered people	3, 25, 26, 36, 39–41
Stagnation	1, 3, 9, 11, 13, 16, 19, 24
Stubbornness	1, 5, 10, 21, 24, 30, 35, 37, 41
Unappreciated people	1, 6, 11–18, 21, 30

| Uncooperativeness | 1, 3–6, 15–17, 21, 25–27, 29, 38, 41 |
| Violent people | 1, 4, 9–11, 15, 21, 23–25, 35, 38, 39, 43 |

Leadership Motivation Plan

Specific challenge (identify)

_____

_____

_____

Ideal Leadership Goals (be specific) date initiated/ desired date of achievement

_____

_____

_____

Progress Report

_____

_____

_____

You Can Be the Motivating Leader!

Twain observed that everyone always talked about the weather but nobody ever did anything about it. Well, like the weather, everyone always talks about unmotivated children, students, employees, or clients. But unlike the weather something can be done about the lack of motivation. Unmotivated or irresponsible people are discouraged. Their discouragement may be seen underneath their apathy, absenteeism, uncooperativeness, closed-mindedness, or myriads of other symptoms. Discouraged people need encouragement to become turned-on, contributing, involved members of the organization. They need a motivating leader.

You can be the motivating leader who is a positive influence on the lives of the members of the organization, nurturing their potential instead of nurturing excuses and coming to grips with the challenges that lie on the. path to your goals. You see disharmony or distrust in the ranks and you build a plan to resolve differences and promote greater understandings; you see people who are down and out and you develop a strategy to lift them up and bring them in so that they can shine the brightest they can; you see alienated, burned-out people who have lost their first day feeling on the job, and you light the fires under them with a flame called "meaning" and "purpose"; you see marginal productivity, and you create a way to communicate high expectations because you believe in them; you see speed limits violated, which affects the total membership, and you confront with class to build, educate, and steer the problem person back on the constructive course; you see people who are overwhelmed with a problem, and you inspire the conviction in their minds and hearts that there is a solution and you take the extra steps together; you see the apathetic and uncooperative person and win them over with a plan to motivate. Observe a number of individuals and become the cohesive glue that that ties them together all in the same direction—headed together for the goal.

When you decide to make a full commitment to be a positive force—that very moment—you take a huge advantage over pessimistic leaders. The advantage is this—never has one human achievement occurred because of a nitpicker, pessimist, or cynic. Every single monumental accomplishment of humankind, from curing polio to placing a flag in the rocky soil of the moon 238,000 miles away happened because of the efforts of optimistic, motivated people inspired by someone to go on and on, refusing to quit, even when in the temporary darkness of night. You can be the motivating leader who sheds that spotlight on your people's possibilities.

Through your warm leadership light, you bring on the morning, and like the blossoms that decorate the trees of spring, they will grow and grow. And in their growth lies your autograph.

Glossary

Chapter 3
Resolving Misunderstandings, Distrust, and Disharmony

1 *Transferring:* Transferring is a leadership approach to minimize jealousies, narrow-mindedness, misunderstandings, and differences based on differing responsibilities. Transferring involves encouraging people to spend some mental time in the private logic of others to experience their world of responsibilities.

2 *Undiagnosing:* Un-diagnosing is the process of unlabeling someone (lazy, paranoid, alcoholic) in instances where the label gives no practical help, and instead, transferring to the person's world and see in their private logic. After the un-diagnosis and the transfer the motivating leader creates a new perception of the person and communicates the new, more productive expectation.

3 *Peeking:* Peeking is an insightful leadership tool that looks beyond a person's surface behavior, emotions, and attitudes to peek at the underlying "real" roots of the discouraged person.

4 *De-escalating:* De-escalating is an approach to prevent a potentially volatile situation by listening with understanding and resisting the tendency to judge. De-escalating occurs when the leader listens by seeing the feelings behind the other person's words.

5 *Exposing:* Exposing involves sharing the pressures and demands that the leader experiences with the other members of the organization. Exposing is designed to assist people to see the situation from a newer, different level perspective.

6 *Linking:* Linking is the process whereby the leader identifies similarities among the membership to bring outsiders in and to help everyone feel linked to the total organization.

Chapter 4
Building People

7 *Re-imaging:* Re-imaging involves developing people by helping them to develop more positive self-images.

8 *Image-Analyzing:* An image-analysis is a leadership technique designed to understand the current self-image of the membership. An analysis reveals limitations based on a person's own definition of self.

9 *Asset-Focusing:* Asset-Focusing is the process whereby a leader identifies and points out "what's right with" the individual or the membership.

10 *Converting:* Converting is a people-building approach in which the leader looks at the negative, unproductive characteristics in a person, sees a positive asset even in the negative and shares the observation.

11 *Special-izing:* Special-izing occurs when a person spots the uniquenesses. These uniquenesses may be the individual's claim to fame.

12 *Best-Foot Forwarding:* Best Foot Forwarding allows people who feel at their worst to re-experience themselves at their best by reinforcing past successes.

13 *Un-assuming:* Un-assuming occurs when the leader

recognizes and doesn't take for granted routine everyday accomplishments of the membership.

14 *Underwhelming:* Underwhelming is the opposite of bowling people over with one's knowledge. Under-whelming builds people because the leader shows respect for their knowledge and turns to them for their contributions.

Chapter 5
Planting Positive Purpose in People

15 *Home-ing In:* Home-ing in is a leadership approach to get into the outside-of-work world of the members to help understand them and give greater meaning.

16 *Meta-job Describing:* Meta-job describing means recognizing people's contribution to themselves, their organization, and society from a higher level to instill greater meaning and purpose.

17 *Winding Up:* Winding up occurs when the leader gets members to look forward to the day or a particular event, or gives them a reason, purpose, or motive to become involved. The leader winds people up by showing them what's in it for them.

18 *Before and Aftering People:* Before and aftering is the process of showing the individual or organization where they were at some point in the past and where they are today.

19 *Un-menializing:* Un-menializing is the leader's reminder to the membership about the importance of its work and how it fits into the organization's goals.

Chapter 6
Create a Winning Feeling with People to Increase Productivity

20 *Respect-ability:* Respect-ability is the leader's overall ability to convey respect and confidence in his or her people.

21 *Delegating:* Delegating involves analyzing the people in the organization to see who would be capable of taking on higher level responsibilities, training them, encouraging them and then celebrating their achievements with them.

22 *"Can" Opening:* "Can" Opening is a leadership approach designed to create a winning feeling in a person by showing the person that he or she is much more capable than previously thought.

23 *Expectation Altering:* Expectation altering is a change in the way a leader views his or her expectations of a member's capabilities and potential. It is a mental switch in the leader's mind, which is then communicated to the specific member.

24 *Changing Spotlights:* Changing spotlights involves communicating positive expectations by taking a risk and giving the challenging responsibility to a previously overlooked member.

Chapter 7
Confronting with Class: Picking People Up Without Stooping Down

25 *Speed Limiting:* Speed Limiting is a leadership approach that defines limits to bring maximum freedom to the total membership and to reduce the anxiety by providing guidelines that create mutual expectations.

26 *Asserting:* Assertive leadership is a balance between timid leadership (die and let live) and aggressive leadership (live and let die). The assertive leader confronts when the speed limits are violated but does not spend his or her time waiting for the violation.

27 *Disciplining:* Disciplining with class is a specific five-step process to deal with offenders of the speed limits.

1. Gather the facts.

2. Set discipline conference goals prior to the meeting.

3. Schedule the discipline conference.

4. Use the ten-step approach to confront with class.

5. Follow up after the conference.

28 De-hiring: De-hiring is the process of breaking ties with a member of the organization when the member has violated speed limits continually, thus indicating that neither the organization's needs are met nor is the individual fulfilled.

Chapter 8
Putting Your People in Second Gear

29 Jonas Salking: Jonas Salking is a leadership approach designed to create the feeling in the membership that "our problems have solutions." This mental attitude orchestrated by a second-gearing leader helps push the membership's minds one step further.

30 Environmental Engineering: Environmental engineering occurs when the leader shapes the people and physical environment in such a way to give a lift to the membership.

31 Talking It Up: Talking it up is a leader's way of using lifting, upbeat, enthusiastic, and hopeful words. The talking-it-up leader knows that words are the propellants that stimulate the minds of the membership to overcome the challenges.

32 Sweet Surrendering: Sweet surrendering is a leadership approach that involves facing reality head-on, accepting things the way they are.

33 Rational Leading: The rational leader assists the membership to see its situations more rationally by overcoming three irrational beliefs:

1. We must be perfect in everything we do.

2. Other people must act the way we think they should.

3. The world must make things easier for us.

34 Opti-realistic Leading: The opti-realistic leader

employs the best of both worlds—optimism and realism.

1. There's a problem that is a challenge to us.
2. Somewhere there is a solution.
3. Let's generate alternatives.
4. Let's find the best alternative.
5. Let's act.
6. Let's evaluate our actions.
7. Employ the same process(1–6).

Chapter 9
Erasing Apathy and Uncooperativeness by Goal-Centered Leadership

35 *Morale Analyzing:* Morale analyzing is a leader's technique to measure the morale of the organization in terms of its feelings of being involved contributors whose ideas are heard.

36 *Goal-Centering* The goal-centered leader keeps his or her mind on the goals, not on one's own ego.

37 *Performing Perfection-ectomys:* Apathy, uncooperatives, fears, and closed-mindedness are related to perfectionism. The motivating leader performs a perfection-ectomy by helping the membership develop the courage to be imperfect.

38 *Crediting:* Crediting is the process of giving open credit to the person who gives an idea.

Chapter 10
Turning Self-Centered Individuals
Into Team Players

39 *Team Theming:* Team Theming is constantly reminding the membership to think *we, our,* and *us* rather than *me.*

40 *Cooperative Focusing:* The cooperative focusing leader highlights cooperation, as opposed to competition, in the membership.

41 *Sociograming:* Sociograming is an approach designed to understand the social structure of the membership to identify leaders, cliques, and mutual relationships. The sociogram helps a leader develop a strategy to build involved team players.

42 *Welcome Mat Weaving:* Welcome Mat Weaving occurs when the leader helps a new member feel welcomed into the team or helps a returning member feel accepted.

43 *Team Esteeming:* Team esteeming is the motivating leader's building morale of the total team, their uniquenesses, achievements, and potential.

Bibliography

Adler, Alfred. *Understanding Human Nature*, New York: Greenberg Publishers, 1927.

Adler, Alfred. *Social Interest*, New York: Putnam, 1939.

Alberti, Robert E., and Michael Emmons. *Your Perfect Right*, San Luis, Obispo: Impact, 1982.

Ansbacher, Heinz, and Rowena Ansbacher. *The Individual Psychology of Alfred Adler*, New York: Basic Books, 1956.

— Bennis, Warren. *The Unconscious Conspiracy: Why Leaders Can't Lead*. Executive Books, 1978.

Brookover, W. B., A. Patterson and S. Thomas. *Self-Concept of Ability and School Achievement*. U.S. Office of Education, Cooperative Research Project 845. East Lansing: Office of Res. & Pub. Michigan St. University.

Buber, Martin. *I and Thou*, New York: Charles Scribner and Sons, 1958.

Cahn, Richard, in personal communications, January, 1983.

Carnegie, Dale. *How To Win Friends and Influence People*. New York: Pocket, 1964.

Cousins, Norman. *Anatomy of an Illness.* New York: Norton, 1979.

Crosby, Philip. *Quality Is Free,* New York: McGraw-Hill, 1979.

Dinkmeyer, Don, and Lewis E. Losoncy. *The Encouragement Book: on Becoming a Positive Person.* Englewood Cliffs, N.J.: Prentice-Hall, Inc., 1980.

Ellis, Albert. *Reason and Emotion in Psycho-Therapy, Seacaucus,* New Jersey: Lyle-Stuart, 1962.

Ellis, Albert. *Executive Leadership: A Rational Approach.* Citadel Press, 1972.

Ellis, Albert and Robert Harper. *A New Guide to Rational Living,* North Hollywood, Calif.: Wilshire Book Co., 1975.

Ferguson, Marilyn. *The Aquarian Conspiracy,* Los Angeles, Calif.: Tarche, 1980.

Festinger, Leon. "A Theory of Social Comparisons Processes." *Human Relations* 7 (1954) 69, pp. 117-140.

Frank, Jerome. *Persuasion and Healing,* Baltimore Johns Hopkins, 1961.

Fromm-Reichman, Frieda. *Principles of Intensive Psychotherapy.* Chicago: University of Chicago Press, 1950.

Glasser, William. *Reality Therapy,* New York: Harper and Row, 1975.

Harak, Ron, in personal communication, March 1984.

Harding, K. L. A. "A Comparative Study of Caucasian Male High School Students Who Stay in School and Those Who Drop Out." Ph.D. dissertation, Michigan State Univ., 1966.

Karrel, Dean, in personal communication, Feb. 1984.

Kirn, Henry, in personal communication, Feb. 1984.

Losoncy Lewis. *Think Your Way to Success,* North Hollywood, Calif.: Wilshire Book Co., 1982.

Losoncy, Lewis. *Turning People on: How to Be an Encouraging Person.* Englewood Cliffs, N.J.: Prentice-Hall, Inc., 1977.

Losoncy, Lewis. *You Can Do It: How to Encourage Yourself,* Englewood Cliffs, N.J.: Prentice-Hall, Inc., 1980.

Losoncy, Lewis, and Donald W. Scoleri. *The New Psycho-Cosmetologists.* Reading, Pa.: PMI Press, 1984.

Maltz, Maxwell. *Psycho-Cybernetics,* North Hollywood, Calif.: Wilshire Book Co., 1960.

Maslow, Abraham. *Motivation and Personality,* New York: Harper and Row, 1954.

Maslow, *The Farther Reaches of Human Nature.* New York: Viking Press, 1971.

May, Rollo. *Freedom And Destiny,* New York: Norton, 1981.

McGregor, Douglas. *The Human Side Of Enterprise,* New York: McGraw-Hill, 1960.

Naisbitt, John. *Megatrends,* New York: Warner Books, 1982.

Ouchi, William. *Theory Z,* New York: Avon, 1982.

Peters, Tom, and Robert Waterman. *In Search Of Excellence,* New York: Warner Books, 1984.

Powers, Robert, and Joanne Hahn. "Resignation or Courage: The Wisdom to See the Difference." Personal and Guidance Journal, 1978, 57 (4), pp. 219-220.

Purkey, William. *Self-Concept and School Achievement,* Englewood Cliffs, New Jersey: Prentice-Hall, Inc., 1970.

Reisman, David. *The Lonely Crowd.* New York: Harper and Row, 1973.

Rogers, Carl R. *On Becoming a Person,* Boston: Houghton-Mifflin, 1961.

Rosenthal, Robert, and Lenore Jacobeen. *Pygmalion in the Classroom,* New York: Holt, Rinehart and Winston, 1968.

Salk, Jonas. *Survival of the Wisest*. New York: Harper and Row, 1973.

Schuller, Robert. *You Can Become the Person You Were Meant To Be*, New York: Pillar Books, 1976.

Schwarz, David. *The Magic of Getting What You Want*, New York: William Morrow and Company, Inc., 1983.

Skinner, B. F. *About Behaviorism*, New York: Knopf, 1973.

Sullivan, James T. in personal communications, April, 1984.

Townsend, Robert. *Up the Organization*, New York: Knopf, 1974.

Ullrich, Robert A. *Motivation Methods That Work*. Englewood Cliffs, New Jersey: Prentice-Hall, Inc., 1981.

Weisinger, Henfrie, and Norman M. Lobsenz. *Nobody's Perfect*, New York: Warner Communications, 1981.

Whyte, William. *The Organization Man*, New York: Simon and Schuster, 1956.

Wilson, Colin. *New Pathways in Psychology*, New York: Toplinger Publishing Co., 1972.

Zastrow, Charles. *Talk To Yourself*, Englewood Cliffs, New Jersey: Prentice-Hall, Inc., 1979.

Zogas, Gust, in personal communications, January, 1984.

Index

Adler, Alfred, 9, 24, 26
Alberti, Raymond, 125
Anatomy of an Illness, 101
Apollo 11, 82
Aquarian Conspiracy, The, 34, 85
Armstrong, Neil, 83
Assertive behavior, 125–28
    vs. aggression, 125–126
        problems with aggression, 127
    case, 126–27
    vs. timidity, 125–126
Asset-focusing, 70–73
    asset list, 71–73
    reasons for, 70–73
Attention-getting:
    attention needs, 29
    by bad behavior, 28–30
    discouraging leader, 30
    lack of feedback as quencher, 28
    misdirected behavior, 28–30
    reasons for, 29
    rerouting, 29

Before-and-aftering, 91–92
Behaviorism, 143
Bennis, Warren, 99
Best, expecting of, use, 101–02
Best-foot-forwarding:
    nature, 77
    slumping hitter, 77
    videotapes as boosters, 78
Brainstorm sessions, 143
Brookover, W. B., 66
Burger chains, 98
Burnout, 8, 90, 93–94

Cahn, Dr. Richard, 29
"Can" opening, 105–07
    common elements, 106–07
    nature of, 106
Categorization of people, 30, 33
Children, need of to be social, 23–24
Communications, decision about, 58
Confrontation:
    action, need for, 114
    advantages, 114
    anxiety, caused by ignorance, 114,
        117
    assistance, needs, 115
    avoidance, negative effects,
        115–16
    challenges to meet, 118
    classy, nature, 112–13
    vs. destructive, 113–14
    discussion, 112
    displaced hostility, 117
    escapism, 117–18
    irresponsibility, detection by
        employees, 116
    leader responsibility, 117
    passive-aggressiveness, 117
    say vs. hear, 113
Converting, 73–74
    nature, 73
    and negative traits, 74
    prison counselor, quoted, 74
Cooperative focusing, 180–82
    vs. competition, 180
    emphasis techniques, 181
    examples, 181–82
    problems with, 180

Courage, nature of, 152
Cousins, Norman, 101
Crediting:
  Carnegie on, 172
  meetings, 173
  names, 173
  problems with, 173
  Reagan on, 172
  rules, 173
  use, 172–73
Criticism:
  reactions to, 174–75
  welcoming of, 174
Crosby, Phil, 98

De-escalating:
  defined, 196
  nature, 53
  paths, 53
  Rogers on, 52–53
De-hiring, 134–36
  discussion, 134–35
  facts to remember, 135
  and motivating leader, 135–36
Delegating, 104–05
  effects, 104
  example, 105
  nature, 104–05
Differences, resolution of:
  blame game, 42–43
  leaders as dependent, 41
  limited group logic, 42
  and private logic, 42
  problems, common, 43
Disciplining, 128–34
  classy confrontation, 132–34
  defense, 132–33
  discussion, 128, 130
  fact gathering, 130
  followup, 134
  goals for conference about, 130–31
  vs. leadership style, 129
  organization, problems to, 133
  positive note, 132
  problem, specificity of, 132
  scheduling conference of, 131–32
Discouraged people, behaviors and
      goals, 31–32
Discouraging leaders:
  characters of, 11–12
  identifying of, 10–12
Disney, Walt, 1
Disneyland, 98
Dominating leader, 63–64
Dreikurs, Rudolf, 24–25

Ellis, Albert, 149, 154
Emmons, Michael, 125
Empathetic listening, 58

Encouraging leaders:
  abilities of:
    burnout, 8
    identifying of, 9
    mutual respect, 8
    and people's social needs, 9
    positive expectations, 8–9
    potential, evocation of, 8
    realism, 9
    recognition of needs by, 9
    steering, 9
    team players, 9
  character exercise about:
    characters, 13–14
    cooperation, 22
    crises, 21–22
    criticism, 21
    ego, 22
    points to remember, 15, 21–22
    positive expectations, 21
    role significance, 21
    strategies to encourage, 16–20
Environmental engineering:
  advertising campaign, 146–47
  board assembly, 145–46
  consultants, 144–145
  media, 148
  music, 147
  people, environment of, 144–45
  physical engineering, 146–49
  positive motivation tapes, 147
  second gearing, 146
Epictetus, 26, 154
Executive Leadership: A Rational
      Approach, 154
Expectation altering:
  employee reorientation, 109
  nature, 107–08
  and responsibility, 107
  and winning feeling, creating of,
      108–09
Exposing, 54–55, 196
  defined, 196
  example, 54–55
  nature, 54
  resistance to, 54
Expression, 59

Failure, reasons for:
  case, 2
  coach, 4–5
  cosmetologist manager, 2
  family business, 3–4
  needs for success, 2–3
  sales management, 4
  and young people, motivation of, 3
Feedback, 28, 164
Ferguson, Marilyn, 34, 85
Festing, Leon, 100

Field Theory, 70
Ford, Henry, 142
Frank, Jerome, 100
From-Reichman, Freida, 100
Funt, Allen, 101

Gardner, John, 86
Glasser, William, 107
Glossary, 195–201
goal-centering, 167–70
    college marketing expert, 168
    ego- vs. goal-centered leaders
        compared, 167
    Goal Thinking approach, 169
    purchaser, case, 169–70
    threatened feeling, 168–69
Goethe, 97

Hahn, Joanne, 152
Hard times, dealing with, 139–40
    case, 140
    recession of 1982, 139
Harding, K. L., 66
Harmony, decision about, 58
Harper, Robert, 149
Heineken, Fred, 98
Home-ing, in, 87–88
    nature, 87

I-You transfer, 58
Image analyzing, 68–70
    membership participation, 69–70
    methods, 68
    observation, 69
In Search of Excellence, 62, 85, 97
Infants:
    exploration by, 23
    openness of, 24
Insensitivity, as discourager, 163–64
    example, 163
    people as "its," 163
Insights of encouraging leader, 25

Jonas Salking, strategy, 142–43
    and cure of pessimism, 142

Kant, Immanuel, 154
Kennedy, John, 1
King, M. L., 1
Kirn, Henry, 10
Know-it-all leader, 62–63

Laughing cure, 101
Leadership:
    discussion, 1–2
    and meaning giving, 85–86
    mistaken beliefs about, 61
Linking:
    common interests, 56

common struggles, 57
defined, 196
family similarities, 56–57
fear of others, 56
groups, leaving of, 55–56
nature, 56
past experience, 56
Lonely Crowd, The, 84

Magic of Getting What You Want,
    The, 35
Maltz, Maxwell, 66–67
Marcus Aurelius, 154
Marriott, Willard Sr., 98
Maslow, Abraham, 10, 154
Meaning and purpose, need for:
    authority, 84
    lack, in modern world, 83–84
    wives, 84
Megatrends, 33, 85
Meta-job describing, 88–90
    dualism, 88–89
    jobs, livening of, 89
    meta-physical, 89–90, 94
    physical, 89–90, 94
Misunderstandings, 59
Morale, 86
Morale-analyzing, 165–67
Mother Theresa, 1
Motivating leader, insights for:
    insights, 38
    points to remember, 38–40
Motivation, 6–8, 80–81, 94–96,
    136–38, 159–61, 174–75,
    187–94
    assertion, 136
    attacks on problems, 136
    challenges, 159
    common challenges, 190–92
    discipline, 137
    employees, clarity about job,
        136–37
    encouragement, 6–7
    environment, 159–60
    goals, 138
    idea generation, 7–8
    leadership, 192–94
    pessimism, 161
    problem prevention plan, 137
    rationalism, 160–61
    specific behaviors, 138
    words, 160

Naisbitt, John, 33, 85
Nash, Edna, 105
New Guide to Rational Living, A,
    149
New Pathways in Psychology, 86
Nietzsche, 86

On Becoming a Person, 52
Opti-realistic leading:
 features of, 141–42
 nature, 141
 pessimism, 141, 158–59
  compared to optimism, 158–59
Organization Man, The, 84
Ouchi, William, 172

Peeking, 48–52, 195
 defined, 195
 Jung on, 48
 nature, 48
 poem on, 48–51
 roots of emotions, 51–52
People building, discussion, 60
Perfectionism:
 ideas on, 171–72
 in leader, 64–65
 private logic, 171
 reasons for resistance, 170–71
Personal & Guidance Journal, 152
Persuasion and Healing, 100–01
Peters, Tom, 62
Peters and Waterman, 97
Phenomenology, 25–26
Placebo effect, 100–01
Popejoy, Fred, 125
Positive purpose, planting of, 82–83
 author, experience of, 82–83
Powers, Bob, 152
Private logic:
 church member, case, 26
 comprehension vs. agreement,
  27–28
 and discouraging leader, 27
 discussion, 25–28
 and encouraging leader, 27
 point of view, sense of behavior
  from, 26
Problem prevention management
  plan, case, 122–24
 bad attitudes, 123
 customers, 122
 employee advancement, 123
 latenesses, 123
Psychocybernetics, 66
Psychotherapy, leadership and
  expectation in, 100
Purkey, William, 66
Purpose, planting of, 86–87
Puskas, Lou, 28

Quality is Free, 98

Rational leading:
 acts of others, 155–56
 irrational words, 157
 irrationality, 155
 perfectionism, 155
 rational vs. irrational, compared,
  156–57
 realism, 154
 self-contradictions, 155
 thoughts, nature, 154
 and universe, expectations about,
  156
Reality Therapy, 107
Recognition of others, 34
Re-imaging, 66–68
 effects, 66
 labels, 67
 self-definition, 67–68
 in students, 66
Reisman, David, 84
Respect-ability, 102–04
 leader's scale for, 102–04
 nature, 102
Retardation of employee, vs.
  encouragement, 34

Salk, Jonas, 142
Schuller, Robert, 99
Schwartz, David, 34
Scoleri, Donald, 134
Second-gearing, 139, 146
Self-determinism:
 active leader outlook, 36–37
 active perspective, 35
 Adler on, 34
 Losoncy on, 35
 passive leader outlook, 36–37
 passive perspective, 35
 self-starting, 35–36
Silence as discourager, 164–65
 examples, 164
 no progress feedback, effects, 164
Skinner, B. F., 77, 143
Social comparison theory, 100
Sociograming, 182–85
 diagram, 183
 insights, 184–85
 making, 183
 nature, 182
 questions answered by, 183–84
Special-izing, 75–76
 claims to fame, 75
 vs. discouragement, 76
 by manager, 75–76
Speed limits:
 and freedom, 119–20
 guidelines for mutual
  expectations, 120–22
 paradigm, 118–19
 use in school, 124–25
Spinoza, Baruch, 142
Spotlights, changing of, 110–11
 example, 110–11
 nature, 110
Subjective views, 25–28

Survival of the Wisest, 142
Sweet surrendering, 152–53
  case, 152–53
  change, 152

Talking it up, words as tools,
  149–52
  discussion, 152
  examples, 149–50
  leadership styles, 150–51
Teacher leadership, and
  expectations:
Team-esteeming, 186–87
  achievements, 187
  team resources, 186–87
  uniqueness, 187
Team players:
  drill instructors, 176–77
  reasons for, 177
  theming, 178–80
  IQ tests, 99
  self-fulfilling nature of, 99–100
Theory Z, 172
Think Your Way to Success, 144
Threatened leader, 62
  Catch-22 situation, 62
  tension, 62
"Touching" of others, 33
Townsend, Robert, 104
Transferring, 44–45, 195
  defined, 195
  and private logic, 44
  work, exchange, 44–45
Turning People On, 25, 64

Un-assuming, 78–79
  nature, 79

*Unconscious Conspiracy, The: Why
  Leaders Can't Lead*, 99
Underwhelming, 79–80
Undiagnosing:
  defined, 195
  effects, 47–48
  nature, 47–48
  and private logic, 46–47
Uniqueness, looking at, 33
Un-menializing, 92–93
  need for, 93
Up the Organization, 104

Waterman, Robert, 62
We vs. I, 178–79
  athletes, 179
  decisions, 179
  messages, 179
Welcome mat weaving, 185–86
  rookies, 185
Whyte, William, H., 84
Wilkins, Gene, 104
Will. *See* Self-determinism
Wilson, Colin, 86
Winding up, 90–91
  and burnout, 90
  children, 91
  soap operas, example, 90
Winning feeling, making:
  command expectations, 99
  vs. losing leaders, 98
  nature, 97

You Can Do It, 35, 155
Your Perfect Right, 125

Zogas, Gust, 79